D0889797

PRAISE FOR
DETERMINED TO BE DAD

"Millennial LGBTQ people are looking at creating families at a much higher rate than previous generations and still face some of the same roadblocks. Steve's story of coming out and then his odyssey of creating his family is a must-read for anyone pondering their own journey of becoming a parent. Steve provides both practical information about the hoops he jumped through during the process and his stories of self-discovery that brought him to the realization that he could be a father."

—Rev. Stan J. Sloan, CEO, Family Equality

"Steve's journey of becoming a dad demonstrates the human experience of wanting to belong and the need for resilience to be our authentic selves. He writes of many intersectional experiences where he finds commonality with different communities and how those experiences have shaped his life. I highly recommend Determined To Be Dad *for anyone facing roadblocks on their journey of self-discovery."*

—Carin Taylor, Chief Diversity Officer, Workday

"As more companies create inclusive policies and cultures that are fully supportive of LGBTQ employees, it is inevitable that more queer people will be creating families. Steve's journey of building his family and navigating his career in corporate America provides a great testament to what's possible when everyone is encouraged to be authentic. LGBTQ professionals considering becoming parents must read this book."

—Erin Uritus, CEO, Out & Equal Workplace Advocates

"Determined To Be Dad *is a page-turner. Two men creating a family faced turbulence and uncertainty. While compassion, determination, and love, might seem like ordinary concepts, when it comes to living them in the face of real life's adversity, it's easy to lose faith. How becoming a loving father to two adopted children, loyal husband, trusted friend, and good citizen created the deeper meaning in his life.*"

—Svetlana Kim, Award-winning *Author of*
White Pearl and I: A Memoir of a Political Refugee,
co-author of *The Last of the Four Musketeers:*
Allen Joe's Life and Friendship with Bruce Lee, and speaker

"The reality is that we all feel included and excluded at various times in our lives. Steve's experiences on both sides of this paradigm have shaped his values and how he shows up in the world. His tender story of coming out to creating his family gives us all hope that we can build the life of our dreams."

—Jennifer Brown, CEO, Jennifer Brown Consulting,
and Author of *How to be an Inclusive Leader:*
Your Role In Creating Cultures of Belonging
Where Everyone Can Thrive

"For me and so many other LGBTQ people, creating a family is a long process of research and planning. It's an exploration of what it means to be a family. Determined To Be Dad *shares the story of Steve's own deeply personal exploration of identity, family, and parenthood. His experiences overcoming the hurdles of building a family will give hope to any aspiring parent.*"

—Dr. Vivienne Ming, Theoretical Neuroscientist, Author,
Co-Founder & Executive Chair of Socos Labs

"*You will celebrate more than one birth as you read this book. Most important to me is the birth of Steve as a gay man, who celebrates the gift of his sexual orientation, rather than tolerate it. Without that joyful marriage of mind and soul, there wouldn't be a good, loving home in which to raise any child. His relationship with Lorevic is another birth, here of a mutual love that welcomes others into its abundance. The birth of his daughter, Kaitlyn, is also the birth of a new family, bound by love. And then, a son, Matthew, making the family whole. You can't help but enjoy participating in this happy, healthy birthing wonder.*"

—Brian McNaught
Author of *On Being Gay*

"*I have known Steve for many years, and I am always impressed with his ability to connect with a broad group of people. Steve's book* Determined To Be Dad *is a tribute to his lifelong desire to become a dad and his belief in the goodness of everyone despite encountering hardships along the way. Steve's open heart and willingness to be vulnerable throughout his adoption journey is a lesson for us all.*"

—Denise (Ajayi) Williams, Author,
President & Cofounder of SVNED

"Steve was amazingly helpful on our show and I was struck by how much he has gone through and how much we can all learn from his experience. Steve's story proves that hope conquers all and that if you want to be a dad you can conquer that too."

—Yan Dekel, Producer and Co-Host of
Daddy Squared: The Gay Dads Podcast

"The foster-to-adopt process in California is both complicated and opaque on many levels with the ultimate goal of keeping the child in a safe and nurturing environment. Steve's conviction to adopt a child from the system speaks to his values and longing for family. Determined To Be Dad will help anyone that is considering the foster-to-adopt process to create their family."

—Supervisor Rafael Mandelman,
District 8 on the San Francisco Board of Supervisors

DETERMINED
TO BE DAD

DETERMINED
TO BE DAD

A JOURNEY
OF FAITH,
RESILIENCE,
AND LOVE

STEVE DISSELHORST

PUBLISH
YOUR
PURPOSE
PRESS

For permission requests, write to the publisher, addressed "Attention: Permissions Coordinator," at the address below.

Publish Your Purpose Press
141 Weston Street, #155
Hartford, CT, 06141

The opinions expressed by the Author are not necessarily those held by Publish Your Purpose Press.

The stories in this book have been written from the Author's recollections. They are not written to represent word-for-word transcripts of conversations or events. Rather, the Author has retold them in a way that evokes the feeling and meaning of what was said. The Author told the story with his own memories and has tried to validate them as much as possible. In all instances, the essence of the dialogue is accurate. However, names and identifying details in some places, have been changed to protect the privacy of the people involved.

Ordering Information: Quantity sales and special discounts are available on quantity purchases by corporations, associations, and others. For details, contact the publisher at orders@publishyourpurposepress.com.

Edited by: Karen Ang
Cover design by: Daliborka Mijailović
Typeset by: Medlar Publishing Solutions Pvt Ltd., India

Printed in the United States of America.
ISBN: 978-1-951591-11-3 (hardcover)
ISBN: 978-1-951591-10-6 (paperback)
ISBN: 978-1-951591-12-0 (ebook)

Library of Congress Control Number: 2020902018

First edition, June 2020.

The information contained within this book is strictly for informational purposes. The material may include information, products, or services by third parties. As such, the Author and Publisher do not assume responsibility or liability for any third-party material or opinions. The publisher is not responsible for websites (or their content) that are not owned by the publisher. Readers are advised to do their own due diligence when it comes to making decisions.

Publish Your Purpose Press works with authors, and aspiring authors, who have a story to tell and a brand to build. Do you have a book idea you would like us to consider publishing? Please visit PublishYourPurposePress.com for more information.

TABLE OF CONTENTS

MY HUSBAND, LOREVIC, and I became parents to our daughter, Kaitlyn, in April 2012. We had only known our daughter's birth parents for a total of eight days and had just met them five days before her birth. After driving six hours from our home in Oakland, we arrived in Torrance, California, at 2 a.m. and went straight to Little Company of Mary Hospital. We had no clue where we would sleep that night and weren't sure how things would unfold, but we were ecstatic to meet our little girl.

The next 24 hours would be the most life-changing experience of our lives. As the morning turned to afternoon, Kaitlyn's birth mother, Lyla, was waiting to give birth and invited us into her room to spend time together. I had knots in my stomach. I was so excited about becoming a parent and nervous about the uncertainty around the adoption. Lyla's family came to visit her and meet us. It was surreal to be at the center of the birthing suite with all of these new family members. In some ways, it was so awkward to be sharing such an intimate moment with people we just met, but it also felt very comforting to be part of a bigger, extended family—all focused on bringing our daughter into the world.

After dinner, things started to change. Lyla began to have contractions. At about 7 p.m., the nurses told us the baby would be coming soon. The nurses and staff prepared the room. Kaitlyn's birth father, Justin, was there by Lyla's side. Lorevic and I were at the head of the bed, talking and waiting. We began the process of bringing our daughter into the world. Over the next five hours, an army of doctors and nurses were coming in and out of the room as the energy and tension ebbed and flowed as the contractions came and went. Those five hours felt like an eternity to us, I can only imagine how it felt for Lyla. We shared stories about our lives and learned lots about Lyla's other children.

After lots of contractions, the obstetrician rushed into the room for the delivery. Lyla encouraged Lorevic to move to the end of the bed. She gave three big pushes, a rush of fluids came flowing out, and our daughter came into the world. The doctor handed her to Lorevic to hold her first. I was quivering with excitement and crying with joy. I took the scissors, and, as my hands trembled, I cut the umbilical cord. Moments later, Lorevic handed Kaitlyn to me. I held my daughter for the first time and my heart skipped a beat. I was filled with adoration and wonder at the sight of her face and the feeling of her body in my arms. For two men, this was the closest we would ever come to giving birth and we felt so honored to be part of her delivery. We fell in love and felt the urge to protect and care for Kaitlyn immediately.

Up until then, this was the greatest joy I had ever felt in my life. Fast forward a few years, and our second greatest joy would arrive.

But becoming a dad wasn't easy. It was a long and difficult journey, filled with self-discovery, acceptance, heartbreak, hope, faith, and resilience.

PREFACE

MY NAME IS Steve Disselhorst. I am gay, cisgender, Caucasian man in my early fifties, raising two amazing children in partnership with the love of my life. I am grateful and honored that you have decided to witness my journey and read my story.

I have led a life of privilege and opportunity. I haven't always been so conscious of all of my blessing, but today I am. I feel incredibly blessed and happy to be leading a life full of love, kindness, strength, perseverance, and faith. I am a father, a husband, a son, a brother, an uncle, a friend, a survivor, a Christian, an activist, a volunteer, a business owner, and now an author.

In my twenties, I felt society's disdain and prejudice about my sexual orientation. During this time, I didn't feel privileged and I saw my plight as a gay man as a flaw that impacted every aspect of my life. Over the years and through endless hours of therapy, I have come to love myself and my individuality. Along this journey, I have gone from feelings of loss and sadness to hope and joy.

Over the last two years, I have faced life-changing events that shook me to my core and made me question what I value, what makes me happy, and how I want to live my life. In September 2017, we finalized the adoption of our son, which was a long, difficult road. During the adoption process, I told myself over and over that if we lost custody of him, I would quit my job and have a greater impact on society. In February 2018, I was diagnosed with prostate cancer and in June 2018, I was laid off from my corporate job.

The cancer diagnosis gave me a deep appreciation for my life and living, and motivated me to write this book. I feel lucky that my cancer was treatable and I can now call myself a survivor. I reflect on the fact that others were not as fortunate as me, and I want to live a fuller life in their memory. Becoming a cancer survivor has pushed me to live every day more fully and like it's my last.

These life events made me think about life in a very different way and really dig deep into myself to really understand more about who I am. There were tremendous lows and incredible highs. I learned to accept things that I could not control and advocate for how I want to be treated and live. I became stronger in my conviction to lead a meaningful life, more in touch with my inner voice, and more grateful for all the amazing gifts in my life. Through these challenges, it became clear to me that God was telling me to have a bigger impact on the world and to throw caution to the wind to live fully. As a gay man who struggled for years with my identity, I have decided to write this book to help others by sharing my dream about becoming a father and creating my family.

It's only since 2015 that the federal government has recognized the rights of same-sex couples to marry. With the rights of marriage, LGBTQ couples now have the legal protections to create families, and more LGBTQ people can dream about a future without limitations. While LGBTQ people have been creating families for many years, it's only recently that it has become part of the mainstream. The next generation of LGBTQ people are thinking about family formation at a much higher rate than my generation. According to the Family Equality Council, there are 3.8 million (77%) LGBTQ millennials who are considering expanding their families in the coming years and 2.9 million (63%) are actively planning to do so.[1]

---

[1] Family Equality Council, "Survey."

My hope is that this book will help others dream about a future that aligns with their heartfelt wishes and desires. I share my journey of becoming a proud gay man and a parent—the internal struggles of self-acceptance and the external acceptance of family, friends, and society. I hope that my story will help others who are fearful of coming out, that my life lessons will help ease others' pain through their own hardships, and that those who dream about creating their own family know that it can be within reach.

PART 1

EARLY YEARS

CHAPTER 1

THE BEGINNING

I ALWAYS KNEW THAT I wanted to be a parent and have a family. It was part of the fabric of my being from the beginning of my life. A family is what made me feel happy and connected to humanity. The intimacy of the touch of my mother holding my hand and comforting me from a scraped knee. The bond with my sister—with whom I shared a room—and the giggles and laughter of our late-night chatter. The predictability of my father arriving home from work for dinner and then falling asleep in his chair. My two older brothers who did everything together. The lessons of grit and perseverance from the grandmother who emigrated on a ship across the Atlantic Ocean. The personal connections with cousins from across the country and around the world. The festivities of life through parties and celebrations. I loved all of this and wanted this for my own family when I grew up. This desire to be a parent felt predetermined, like the color of my eyes and the way I walked.

I grew up in an Irish and German Catholic family. My parents, Pat and Lou Disselhorst, had a short courtship after meeting at the Chicago Young Christian Worker's Dance in Waukegan, Illinois. It was love at first sight, and they got married. They quickly started a family with the birth of my oldest brother, Bill, within the first year of their marriage. My second brother, Bob, was born one year later, my sister, Julie, two years later, and finally me, two years later. There were four of us within five years—an infant, a two-year-old, a four-year-old, and a five-year-old. My two oldest brothers were inseparable, and my sister and I became very close. Shortly after I was born in Grant Hospital in Chicago, my parents moved us to Skokie—a middle-class suburb outside of Chicago—to buy a house and create an independent life.

We lived in three different homes over the course of my childhood. Our first home on Kilbourn Street was less than a block from the Skokie Swift Railroad, which connected Skokie to downtown Chicago. It was a small two-story bungalow with a semi-finished second floor where Bill and Bob shared a room. Julie and I shared a room across from my parents' bedroom on the first floor. The neighbors on the block were incredibly close-knit, and Tom, my best friend from this period in my life, is still a close friend. These relationships made us more like extended families than neighbors. Tom and I were inseparable for most of our early childhood.

By the time I was in third grade, we outgrew this tiny bungalow and moved to Lincolnwood, the adjacent town. We had a bigger home with a large backyard and side lot, which felt very cushy to a child. We did not change schools or churches and, instead, commuted back and forth. While we loved the new house, we felt like misfits in this new neighborhood, estranged from the community. After a short time, my parents decided the additional space wasn't worth the loss of our connections, and they began to look for a new house close to our church in Skokie, St. Peter's Catholic Church.

Within a year and a half, we moved back to Skokie, walking distance from our church and school, across from Lorel Park. It was a modest Cape Cod on a corner lot. When we first moved in, my parents occupied the bedroom on the first floor across from the kitchen, my brothers and I shared a large bedroom on the second floor, and my sister had her own room across from us. It could fit all six of us, yet there was no room to spare.

When my grandmother became elderly, she moved into our home. One of my first cousins also lived with us for a while. With eight people living in a house with one and a half bathrooms, there was always a line to take a shower. It felt really small, like we were living on top of each other. In order to make room for my grandma, my brothers, my cousin, and I moved to the basement. There were four beds lined up from one end of the room to the other. During this time, there was absolutely no personal space.

Both of my parents came from families of five children and large extended families. My maternal grandmother, Nana, emigrated from Ireland in the early 1900s. She was raised on a dairy farm in County Kerry in the western part of Ireland and was one of seven children. There were too many mouths to feed, so she was forced to leave her home when she was around 14 years old to find a better life in America. She traveled across the Atlantic Ocean with other Irish immigrants and landed at Ellis Island in New York. As the matriarch of my mother's extended family, she was loved and revered by her children, grandchildren, and almost everyone who she encountered. She was courageous, determined, strong, and dedicated to her family. Nana was a formidable figure in my childhood and someone whom I admired greatly.

My paternal grandparents were both of Irish and German heritage. We were never close to Grandma and Grandpa D, and when we were together, it was uncomfortable and strained. Grandpa D was an angry, vindictive, and nasty man who treated many people poorly, including my father. Although, my dad had a difficult childhood, he bounced back and went on to become a salesman, father, and grandfather. He tried to be the most loving and kind human being and not reflect any of the characteristics of his father.

Despite my parents facing obstacles during their own childhoods, they provided a very loving and secure family life for us. It was a typical, lower-middle class upbringing—a large family with almost no money for anything beyond the basics of food and shelter.

There were no fancy TVs and games. In fact, for many years, we only had one black-and-white TV in the basement. We weren't allowed to watch

TV and, in all honesty, the TV was terrible so I didn't really want to watch it. We used our imaginations to create our own games and fun. I spent most of my time outdoors when I wasn't in school—playing in the park, riding bikes with Tom, and exploring the world around me.

There were no summer camps or extracurricular activities. In our family, we shared everything. Most of my older brothers' clothes were passed on to me, so I wore hand-me-downs for much of my early years. I recall needing new gym shoes when I was in the sixth grade, and the effort of convincing my dad to spend the money on them. He wanted me to use my brothers' hand-me-downs but they didn't fit me. He eventually relented, but it made me realize how much my dad stressed out about providing for his family. This experience made me want to get my own job so I wouldn't have to ask him again.

On one hand, I loved being part of a big family with all the connections, sharing, and love. On the other hand, the lack of personal space and the chaos of a large family crammed into a relatively small living space was stifling to me. Nothing belonged to me, and everything was collective. This feeling permeated my identity as well. I felt that my family identity was more important than my own identity. While we all expressed some uniqueness, that was secondary to our family identity. Later in life, I found it difficult to figure out who I was because I was so aligned to my family identity.

Despite our modest lifestyle, my parents always found a way for us to go on family vacations. We drove across the Midwest and the Rocky Mountains to find places where we could vacation on a shoestring budget. When I was very young, we spent most of our vacations in a tent camping. We didn't have the money to rent hotel rooms, so we all piled into one giant tent and slept on the ground. I loved the closeness of those tent vacations, but the terrain was usually rocky, and it was almost impossible to get everyone to sleep at the same time. And the smell of all those people in close quarters was no fun.

But I loved our vacations for many reasons. During these vacations, I encountered all kinds of people, which excited me and made me feel unfettered. I loved being outside all the time, spending days swimming and playing and evenings around the campfire. As we got older, we started to take ski vacations to the Rocky Mountains and abandoned the cramped tent. I loved these vacations because I got to experience peaks and nature in a very different way. I remember driving from Nebraska into Colorado and then starting to see the mountains. We were completely in awe of the size and shape of the mountains and the change in geography. I have many fond memories of the six of us climbing into our station wagon and driving to Colorado or Wisconsin or Arkansas or many other places. We never flew anywhere, and we were always together. Our family vacations gave me a vision into a world divergent from my existence.

Our Catholic faith was central to our lives. We went to church every Sunday and we celebrated all religious holidays. God was the center of our lives and the principles of a Catholic life were fundamental to my childhood. The scripture teaching of "love thy neighbor as thyself" was the basis of how we interacted with our family, friends, community, and the outside world. These were the values that I learned at an early age and the values that I brought forth with me in my life as I grew older.

My father went to a seminary high school and then started in the priesthood as a young man. He spent one year as a seminarian before deciding it wasn't for him. He left to teach and later become a salesman and then a husband and father. While he gave up a formal religious life, he carried the rituals, doctrine, and deference to the Catholic Church hierarchy with him. While I knew he had a profound faith, I saw his interpretation of religion more about rules, structure, and following the edicts of the governing church. He attended church every Sunday and on all the holy days. He frequently volunteered his time for church fundraisers. At least once per month, he volunteered to make donuts after Sunday mass to raise funds for the school. He placed his responsibilities to his church high on his list of priorities.

On the other hand, my mother was less dogmatic, yet demonstrated a profound faith. I remember so clearly going to church with her and watching her pray. She would kneel down when she entered the pew and she remained silent while she prayed. She held onto my hand so tightly. I felt the blood rushing through her veins when she prayed, and it felt like time stood still. Mom was transcended from that pew to another place with God. When I saw her in turmoil, she relied on her belief in a higher power for strength and to bring meaning to her situation. She persevered through her hardships with her connection to God. I learned the meaning of faith from her, which has helped me through so much in my own life.

Mom and Dad valued family over everything else. Both of my parents had big hearts and were actively involved in our extended family, our community, and our church. Relationships with others were the foundation of our family. As a family, we always ate together, prayed together, did chores together, and shared our lives together. Dinnertime was sacred in our house. We were not allowed to answer the phone or leave the table without permission. Dinnertime was the one time of day where we all came together to connect and hear about our individual lives. We talked about issues both big and small. While all six of us crowded around our kitchen table, we shared our hopes and dreams as well as our failures and setbacks. It wasn't all hunky-dory. There were lots of disagreements and, in some cases, intense fights. Despite the tumultuous times at the table, this time of connection and building relationships was an essential formative experience for me.

On my mother's side of the family, I have 18 first cousins, and on my father's side, I have six first cousins. Our weekends and holidays were spent visiting relatives, celebrating birthdays, graduations, confirmations, baptisms, weddings, and life. Family and physical closeness were as familiar to me as the hair upon my head. The sense of love, care, and concern were always part of our daily existence.

Since Nana lived with us, she became part of the fabric of my daily life. We spent lots of time together when she lived with us during my junior high and high school years, and she and I became very close. She told people that I was her favorite grandson, which felt very awkward with all my other cousins and siblings. Looking back on that time in my development, I now realize that I unconsciously used my relationship with my grandmother to avoid dealing with my sexuality and identity. She had her own room in our cramped home, and I spent endless hours there, avoiding my siblings and the boys from my class. Her bedroom faced the park where many of my peers were playing sports. I would sneak a peek at them through the blinds and hope they wouldn't notice me. While I didn't know how I was different, I knew that I didn't want to play sports with them and felt afraid to be myself around them.

Nana and I played go-fish, gin rummy, and other card games frequently. We baked Irish soda bread together from the recipe in her head. Together, we watched her color TV—which was off limits to everyone else without her permission. We became best friends of sorts. We went to dinner together at the local restaurant and didn't include anyone else. Besides avoiding my issues, I was learning from her about how to get through life with difficulties. She shared many of her stories of perseverance, grit, and faith that helped form me into the person I am today.

This idea of connection to our roots and family formed a great deal of my identity growing up. Almost all of my aunts and uncles were married and had large families of their own that could carry on the family line. There was only one uncle on my dad's side who didn't have a family. He lived in San Francisco and had been a flight attendant. There was almost no talk about him, and he was a virtual mystery. On my mom's side, I had one aunt who was divorced and had one child who was in and out of foster care. Otherwise, all my aunts and uncles were married and had children.

Heterosexual, married family life was the expectation for my community. Every kid in my elementary school had parents who were still married. All of my parents' friends were married with the exception of two—one of them was a Catholic priest and the other was my mother's high school friend. There were virtually no images or role models of anything other than traditional family life. Conformity to societal expectations and family were the norms.

I loved my commonality with all of these family members—siblings, cousins, aunts, and uncles. Even though we lived in different cities and had different experiences, we shared blood and a familiar background. I wanted the same for myself when I became an adult. I tried to imitate my parents and all the family around me. At that time, I wanted to have children who were a reflection of me, my heritage, and my bloodline. These values formed the basis of my identity for my relationships in the future. My life centered around family, and this is how I envisioned my future.

CHAPTER 2

ESCAPING CORPORAL
PUNISHMENT

I FELT A STRONG pull to conform to the community and school norms, which stifled my unique personality. I went to St. Peter's Catholic School, which was the center of our lives and helped form many of my early lessons. Many of the teachers in the school were nuns. The school administrators, including the principal, were also nuns, which meant they had the authority to do what they wanted without checks and balances on their power. Just as some Catholics believe that the pope has divine and supreme authority over the Roman Catholic Church, these nuns had complete authority over St. Peter's School.

Most of the families were Irish, English, Scottish, German, Polish, and from other Northern European backgrounds. Italians were considered exotic. While the community was kind and loving, they were cautious of outsiders. They demonstrated their kindness through acts of giving and helping—as long as you fit into the group. The homogenous nature of the neighborhood brought me comfort on some level because neighbors were similar to me, which created predictability and commonality. On a less conscious level, it was stifling. Even at a young age, I longed for people unlike me, faraway places, and different experiences.

At school, there was the typical childhood banter making fun of people who were different. The kids often made fun of other kids because they were left-handed or wore glasses. My brother Bob was teased ruthlessly for having big ears. At St. Peter's School and the surrounding community, the banter took a more unfriendly tone and was part of a broader distrust of strangers. I recall hearing hateful rhetoric toward blacks, Jews, and homosexuals while I was in elementary school. Even though we lived in a village with a high percentage of Jewish people, we did not have Jewish friends or neighbors. I recall classmates making fun of Jews and creating a Hitler Youth Group to espouse our Christian superiority.

While my family taught me to treat everyone with respect and dignity, I could see something different with some of the kids and the community around me. Anyone who didn't attend our Catholic school was considered suspicious. On Saturdays, Catholic kids attending public school would come to St. Peter's for Confraternity of Christian Doctrine (CCD). CCD provided religious education to Catholics who did not attend parochial school. Every Monday, we came back to school and looked for these kids' wrong doings. We would tell the teachers that they stole things out of our desks. We were distrustful of them because we thought they were not as pure in their Catholicism.

When I went to play dates at the house of one of my classmates, his father spewed hateful words like the N-word, and said things like blacks were lazy. I always recoiled when I heard these words. It always felt wrong to me, but I felt powerless to speak up to his dad. Underneath that discomfort, I somehow knew that I, too, was different but I didn't really understand homosexuality.

At a few points in my early years, I participated in this vicious behavior to fit in and not call attention to myself. I roamed the neighborhood with Rick, David, and some other boys, and went to the house of an older boy who we thought was weird. He was an only child, a loner, nerdy, and slightly effeminate. He acted different than us and, therefore, was a target. We tried to get him to come outside as we taunted him. Some of the boys called him a faggot. I didn't even really understand what it meant, but I knew it was hurtful and wrong. I quickly learned that when I tried to speak up for outsiders, I would then become suspicious in my friends' eyes. I learned early that fitting into the group culture would cause me less pain and ridicule. I learned how to "pass" and wear a mask. I also started to try to avoid these types of situations and hide from these boys when I thought they wanted to engage in hostile behaviors.

Around this time, I wanted to dress as a girl or woman. I didn't know what it meant, but I knew I liked it and wanted to explore it. My Aunt Gayle lived two blocks away from our house. She was divorced from my mother's brother and she was raising five children. Aunt Gayle was my mother's best friend and we were always spending time at her house. Aunt Gayle was comfortable with my dress-up play and gave me positive reinforcement to experiment with this behavior. I was afraid to dress up in women's clothes in front of my parents or siblings. I didn't think they would accept it. I can see now that it's through this suppression of our true identities that we start to question if we can trust ourselves and the people around us. In many cases, this feeling of distrust and lack of safety as a child made me pull back from being myself and connecting with others. I was afraid to show others my true self because I was afraid that they would reject me or hurt me.

In the fourth grade, things came to a head for our family at our Catholic school. My mom finally got fed up with the physical discipline and abuse at the hands of the nuns and teachers. My mom was a volunteer school nurse a couple of days a week and she observed some of the harsh behavior. My brother Bob experienced serious discipline from the music teacher when she locked him in a closet for misbehaving in class. The heater was located in the closet and the temperature was suffocating. He was locked in the closet for over an hour and emerged from that class feeling sick and scared. While Bob had a mischievous streak, he didn't deserve such inhumane treatment. When my mother learned about this situation, she became very angry.

My fourth-grade teacher, Ms. Potsdam, was not a nun but had tenure due to her over 20 years of service. She was incredibly strict and very mean. One day, I misbehaved in her class. I can't remember exactly what I did, but I remember her vicious response. She came over and pulled my arm to remove me from the classroom. She dug her nails into my arm and broke the skin. I started bleeding and the blood kept coming for a while. I was startled by the brutality of the interaction and scared that she might hurt me again. When I went home and told my mother, she was outraged. She had seen what they had done with Bob and now me. The next day, Mom went to speak with the principal, Sister Theresa, to demand that Ms. Potsdam stop grabbing me. Sister Theresa supported Ms. Potsdam's actions and ignored my mom's request for change. She reminded my mom that corporal punishment was acceptable in Catholic schools. My mother's instincts to protect her children and stand up to power came out quickly. When she realized she couldn't change the institutional brutality, she decided to take Julie and me out of St. Peter's and moved us to the local public school. Julie transferred to Lincoln Junior High and I transferred to Edison Elementary School for the fifth grade.

When I left St. Peter's School, I was heartbroken. I was losing a tight-knit group of friends, and through this change, I was labeled different. I felt ostracized from Rick and David, who were my best friends at St. Peter's. I was furious with my parents for taking me out of that school. I grieved for the loss of these friendships. I didn't want to disrupt those ties, despite the toxic environment.

On the other hand, I was also relieved to get away from abusive teachers and offensive behaviors. These feelings of sorrow and loss on one level and happiness and excitement on another level would become a familiar pattern throughout my life. This change taught me perseverance and resilience.

At Edison Elementary, I was exposed to students from outside my religion and ethnicity. My 24-member class was filled with Jewish and Indian kids who couldn't care less about Christmas, let alone about my Irish Catholic heritage. At the time, this was the most profound change in my life—a change that would eventually enable me to become the person I am today. In this setting, I started to embrace people of difference and celebrate that the world was much bigger and more interesting than my community. This experience helped me consider a different future and gave me the strength to choose an unconventional path for myself. While I didn't know I was gay at the time, I learned empathy and compassion for people, and perseverance to help me in the future.

Once at the new school, I realized that most of these kids had been in the same class since kindergarten. When I started there, I was an outsider, and I was isolated and lonely. I walked home from school every day for lunch with my mother and watched the soap opera *Days of Our Lives* to distract me from what I was experiencing at school. I longed for this one-on-one time with Mom while my siblings were at school.

It took me a long time to break into a new group of friends and, for a long time, I had no friends at Edison. On top of being friendless, I was being bullied by a girl in my class. Vera was a brash, loud, and aggressive Greek girl who made fun of my Catholicism and what I wore. She towered over me as she taunted me. I felt physically intimidated by her and afraid to speak up about her bullying. I struggled with loneliness and sadness at this time. In hindsight, I am grateful that I experienced these feelings early in my life because it taught me how to handle the changes that would come later in life. I learned how to be alone and follow my heart.

At Edison, there were many Jewish families. While I grew up in one of the most Jewish suburbs of Chicago, I didn't know any Jewish people until I arrived at this school. In the late 1970s, Skokie was a community of around 68,000 people. During my first year at Edison, there was a horrible incident that would have a significant impact on the rest of my life. The Illinois neo-Nazi party wanted to hold a rally at Skokie City Hall to espouse their hateful, racist, and anti-Semitic beliefs.[2] At that time, Skokie had one of the highest percentages of Holocaust survivors—about 7 to 8% of the population had survived. I remember seeing the numbers that had been tattooed onto the arms of people who lived through the concentration camps. My fifth-grade teacher, Ms. Edith, told our class about the horrors of losing many family members to the Holocaust. She was terrified of facing the neo-Nazis at the rally and talked about leaving town to escape it. But she also talked about her responsibility to shed light onto their rhetoric and stand up to the ideology that had decimated her family. She felt a moral obligation to be involved despite her terror.

At the time, I didn't fully understand what it all meant. Some members of the community were saying that the neo-Nazis should be permitted to gather and express their First Amendment rights to freedom of speech. I didn't yet understand our Constitution or democracy and didn't want to see Ms. Edith in pain. I couldn't understand how people could kill others because of their faith or race. That kind of hate was contrary to what I had learned from my family. I was starting to put together in my head that people acted violently and hateful toward people who were different. While I hadn't experienced physical violence firsthand in my community, there were verbal attacks toward strangers. I realized that it was essential to speak out against this hate because complicity could create more hatred. And deep down inside, I knew I was not like everyone else, and I was terrified that someone would find out and hurt me.

My first year at Edison was a challenging year of significant change and transformation. This change would mark the beginning of a new chapter in my development and identity. I started to feel more comfortable being myself and meeting others who were different from me. For the remainder of my education, I stayed in the public school system, which provided me with safety and encouraged me to explore my inner voice.

---

[2] Stone, "Nazis."

As I went through junior high and high school, I expanded my relationships broadly. While I continued to show up as an Irish Catholic boy, I forged connections and networks across different groups. At Lincoln Junior High School, I became very close with many classmates who were Jewish. I became friends with a boy named Alan who lived two blocks from me. He was my first non-Catholic friend. Alan and I became very close over the years and we remain close today.

Through my friendship with Alan, I was exposed to a world of difference. His parents were a far cry from mine. They were very open-minded, direct, and, in some cases, brash. His father Herb would ask me directly which girl I liked and thought was pretty. He wanted to know about my attraction to women. I shied away from conversations with him. In the sixth grade, Alan and I became business partners. Alan had a bustling car washing business and I started working with him. We expanded our business and started cleaning offices and painting houses and offices. I spent many hours at his home with his mom, Bobbi, and she and I had many in-depth conversations. Many times, she challenged my beliefs and forced me to think outside of my world view. During one of those conversations, while Alan was watching TV, I told Bobbi that when I grew up that I was going to marry a nice Catholic girl. She challenged me by asking, "What if you are attracted to a girl and you don't know her religion?" I responded that once I found out that she was not Catholic, then I wouldn't proceed with the relationship.

During my sixth-grade summer vacation when my parents, Julie, and I went to Disney World, I found myself gazing into beautiful blue eyes. Those eyes excited me and I couldn't take my gaze away from them. I realized those eyes belonged to a boy and I immediately told myself that I couldn't do it again. I didn't know anyone else who felt same-sex attraction, and I thought it was not possible for me. I was programmed at an early age to see myself as heterosexual and attracted to people from my background.

During junior high, I was invited to more than 30 bar and bat mitzvahs and learned the rituals of Judaism. In fact, I started to learn the Torah and was able to actively recite the first few prayers during the services. I became envious of my Jewish friends for their celebration of their transition into adulthood. I thought to myself, "How cool is it to have a day where you are the center of attention and everyone is showering you with love and joy at your bar mitzvah?" I felt cheated by Catholic rituals, which celebrated everyone together. As my Catholic Confirmation approached and I became closer with Alan and his family, I wanted to demonstrate my solidarity with my Jewish friends. For Confirmation, I was expected to select a Confirmation name of my choosing. I had always liked the Irish name Erin and had often fantasized about changing my first name to Erin. With my newfound appreciation for Judaism, I decided to use the Hebrew spelling and chose Aaron as my Confirmation name. I felt so proud of myself for integrating my growing appreciation of the world outside of my family. I also invited Alan and his family to the Confirmation. They had become so instrumental in my development and I wanted to share with them this important milestone in my faith journey.

I celebrated Hanukkah and Passover with friends. These relationships with my Jewish friends helped teach me what it felt like to be an outsider and not part of the mainstream culture. From these relationships, I observed the feelings of hurt, pain, and suffering from hatred and bigotry. I listened intently to my friends' parents and grandparents talk about the hate of the Nazis that destroyed their families. From these stories, I learned empathy and compassion for those who face discrimination. I learned to speak up against hatred. I learned the close bonds that come from being in a minority group and how minority groups stick together to protect themselves against the dominant culture. These experiences showed me people are resilient and can be happy while facing discrimination and bias. It gave me a light into a world that would become my future. It gave me hope for a future that would enable me to explore my true identity.

It was through these expanding relationships that I became an ambassador of sorts. I was not aligned with one group of friends, and I identified with people from all walks of life. I found that I could navigate across groups of people with different experiences and I could find common ground among a variety of people. I loved being able to relate to people from divergent backgrounds.

CHAPTER 3

GROWING UP

D URING JUNIOR HIGH, I started working and earning money. I got a job at Judy's Hallmark Card Shop breaking down boxes, stocking cards, and cleaning up. I worked closely with Judy, a funny woman who always made me feel respected and special. She loved to laugh and have fun while working. While working at Judy's, I got another job next door at Dennis's, which was a men's clothing store. This job gave me insight into men buying nice clothing and taking care of themselves. I loved this job because the clothes were beautiful and the men who worked there were well-dressed, coiffed, and worldly. As part of my compensation, they gave me fancy ties and nice shirts. I loved the way I felt when I was there in the presence of these men.

These jobs served a couple of purposes. First, earning money gave me independence and the ability to dream about life outside the community. I saved for college and was able to buy things for myself. It helped me with my self-esteem and helped me contemplate that I might have an identity outside my family. Second, working and being busy helped me repress my attractions and sexuality. While some of my friends were out flirting with girls and acting on their attractions, I was working to keep myself away from those feelings. My Irish grandmother always told us, "Idle hands are the devil's workshop." I kept busy so I could hide from what was bubbling up inside of me.

In junior high, I delved into my Spanish classes and dreamed of a life outside of America. I had started Spanish in sixth grade with a mandatory introductory class with Ms. Johnson. She was a large Caucasian woman who came alive when she spoke Spanish. She seemed so exotic to me. When I was selecting elective classes for the seventh grade, I wanted as much exposure to Spanish as possible. I continued with Spanish in eighth grade. Ms. Johnson talked about Spanish immersion programs in Mexico and Spain, which lit me up. I kept saying to myself, "I want to explore another way of living." In the eighth grade, Ms. Johnson took us on a field trip to a Spanish restaurant in Evanston. It was the first time I was introduced to Spanish food and culture. I loved it and couldn't wait to experience it again. I wondered why there weren't more Spanish and Latin people living in my neighborhood.

When I spoke and listened to Spanish, I was able to express a different part of myself. I felt freer and more comfortable. Spanish enabled me to put on a costume and become a different person. It gave me insight into cultures different from my own and gave me hope for a more diverse world. The *joie de vivre* of the Latin cultures was a welcome change from my Irish and German upbringing of order and rigidity. My passion for Spanish and exploring Latin cultures would continue throughout my life and be a great source of joy.

By the time I started high school, this habit of staying busy and running from myself was well entrenched. I began to play football in the fall, gymnastics in the spring, and I was recruited to join wrestling. I played football for only one season. I had joined to prove my masculinity and bond with the other guys. I felt if I could get through the first season that it would become easier and I would become more masculine. We started practices in August before the academic year started. It was 90 degrees outside with high humidity. I got so nauseated and dehydrated. I hated it but pushed myself to keep going. I loved the tight uniforms and the shoulder pads made me feel strong and macho. But I never knew where to line up for the games and I was always messing up on the field. One of my friends, Sam, got mad at me on many occasions for my multiple errors, like dropping the football, and he berated me for not understanding the game. I felt stressed out during practice and couldn't wait for it to finish. After the first season, I decided it wasn't for me.

In Lincoln Junior High, I was on the wrestling team and won almost all of my matches. When I went to Niles West High School, my teachers and friends encouraged me to join the team. The wrestling coach tried to recruit me for the team. I heard rumblings from some of my friends to stay away from him. He tried to pressure me into joining the team and, with each request, I felt more creeped out by him. He kept saying, "I saw you wrestle last year and you have the skill to go to the state championship. I can make you a great wrestler." His persistent efforts freaked me out and I never joined the wrestling team.

Instead, I joined the gymnastic team, which became my passion and savior over the next four years. It gave me the opportunity to compete against myself and not engage with the jocks. The head coach, Mr. Burkel, took me under his wing and coached and mentored me over the years. I didn't have a natural athletic talent for gymnastics, but he taught me persistence, patience, and grit. These lessons helped me build self-confidence and prepare for future transitions.

After finishing sports, I went home for a quick meal and headed out to my evening job from 6:30 to 9. I worked at Lou's Pharmacy, a block from our church. I loved this job because it gave me status and independence. It felt like an upgrade from the cleaning and stocking jobs I had previously. I worked the cash register at the front of the store. I was out of Lou's sight and I had more autonomy. I met customers who were buying toothpaste, candy, and other over-the-counter items. At times, friends would come into the store with their parents and they were surprised to see me working behind the counter and handling money. Many of them envied me for having a job. Lou also gave us great snacks at times and, occasionally, I stole candy and lottery tickets. This is where my affection for Reese's Peanut Butter Cups started. After a long day, I would arrive home and finish my homework. My days were packed and it left me no time to pay attention to my body or my attractions. In high school, I was also very engaged in school activities like the student council. I took a woodworking class and driver's education.

On the weekend days, I worked at the pharmacy or washing cars with Alan, and then during the evening, I went to parties and drank as another way to escape from myself. I had almost no time to explore any other identity. On the outside, I looked like the model teenager. I was overachieving and people were praising me for all my accomplishments. On the inside, I wasn't sure what I was feeling, but I was trying to get away from anything related to my sexuality and identity. I kept my head down. I worked hard and played hard. The busyness and external validation were ways for me to be a "good boy" and repress anything that didn't fit into that persona.

I began drinking beer in my sophomore year of high school. I rode my bike to parties with Alan since he lived two blocks away. Alan and I would alternate between one of us riding the bike while the other drank beer. Once at the party, we drank to excess. As we got older, we started to drink hard liquor—tequila, vodka, whisky, and anything else we could get our hands on. We had a great time and did lots of crazy things. Our group of friends expanded, and I became close with Eugene and Tom, who became lifelong friends. We had access to alcohol and I used it to avoid feeling.

During these years, everyone was exploring their sexuality. I wasn't interested in girls but wanted to fit in with my friends. I pursued relationships with girls even though deep down, I didn't want them. Part of the reason I drank was to give me the courage to flirt and seek sexual activity with girls even though it wasn't what I truly wanted. During these parties,

I drank a lot to pursue the "hottest" girl and to try to make out with her. I didn't mind the flirting with the girls, and I really liked the attention I got from the other guys when I was successful in connecting with a girl.

One fall weekend, Alan's parents were out of town visiting relatives in St. Louis. Alan didn't go with his parents and decided to throw a toga party. We invited our group of friends and planned a low-key night of drinking beer and hanging out. Someone from our group leaked the party to all the kids from our class and someone from Niles North High School, the other major high school in our village. While we planned for a party of 20 to 30 friends, it turned into this epic out-of-control party. During this party, I made out on the roof with one of the hottest and most uppity girls in our class, Lisa. This interaction and the gossip about it helped my reputation and kept everyone under the impression that I was straight. This party was a blast, but it got so out of hand that we called one friend's parent to come to the house and kick everyone out. Despite all this drinking and partying, my parents were oblivious to what I was doing. They thought I was the model teenager.

For many LGBTQ people who grew up in the 1970s and 1980s, we lived an early existence of not understanding ourselves and not understanding how we fit into the world. During our formative years in school, we didn't have any role models of LGBTQ people, and we couldn't understand our differences. This experience is unlike that of people of color, religious minorities, people with disabilities, and other minorities. In some cases, other minorities are surrounded by people similar to them, despite the harsh realities of the dominant culture. However, in many instances, queer youth feel different but can't put words to it and can't find others with those differences to affirm their experiences. Then there are the times that we express our differences and we are instructed to act differently to cover them. For me, I was alone in my search to understand myself and my difference.

In the midst of all my drinking and trying to fit into the guy culture, I longed to get out of my little world and see if things were different elsewhere. During my junior year of high school, there was an opportunity to participate in a foreign exchange program. This program entailed hosting a student from Germany and going to Germany for one month. The eligible students for the study abroad program were German language students. I desperately wanted to participate in the program but wasn't a German language student. There was no similar program for Spanish language students at my high school. When I inquired about the program, I learned that the cost was prohibitive for me at the time. I was devastated. I had never left the United States and was desperate for an offbeat experience. I begged the program director to allow me to be involved and help me with a scholarship. He rebuffed me until there weren't enough host families for all the German students, and then allowed me to participate in the hosting aspect of the program. I pleaded with my parents to host one student for the summer. After some negotiating, they relented.

After my junior year, Markus, who was from Hanover, Germany, arrived for one month during the summer. It turned out to be a mixed blessing. The student was not a big fan of American life, and it became clear over the summer that he was looking to escape his parents. He had no interest in learning English or learning about the culture. He was very critical of my mother and how we lived. He was an atheist and questioned our religion. Our experience as a host family turned out to be a negative experience for our family, but it jolted me out of an America-first mentality. While I disliked Markus, it didn't dissuade me from wanting to go to Germany.

After hosting the foreign exchange student and becoming involved in the cohort, I was able to convince the director to include me on the trip for the following summer. My next challenge was funding the trip. I had worked since I was 12 years old and had savings earmarked for college. My parents did not have any extra funds to help pay for the entire trip. I was able to negotiate some help from my parents and a scholarship with my school. Then, I worked extra hours at my various jobs to come up with the funds.

In the summer after my senior year of high school, I traveled to Germany for the first of many trips to foreign lands. This trip opened my eyes to a new world with more diversity and gay people. My host family's next-door neighbors were a lesbian couple. I was so excited about the normalcy of these queer people living next door. In all of my life, I had no personal relationships with LGBTQ people. Almost all the information I had learned about LGBTQ people was negative and scary. While living with the host family, I experienced no words or actions of homophobia or discrimination toward these lesbians. This couple received the same respect, kindness, and connection as anyone else. I returned from Europe and left for college with the beginning of a new perspective about the world and queer people.

CHAPTER 4

FROM LOUNGE LIFE
TO FRAT LIFE

W HEN I WENT off to the University of Iowa, my parents spent the weekend helping me adjust to my new home. The University of Iowa is in a beautiful southeastern Iowa city along Interstate 80 in the middle of cornfields along the Iowa River. It is a picturesque town with a safe and friendly environment where my parents felt comfortable leaving me to start college. I recall shedding lots of tears when they got back in the family station wagon on Sunday morning to return to our family home 200 miles away. I was terrified of being on my own. I had been so attached to my family for my entire childhood.

When I first arrived in Iowa City to begin my freshman year, my brother was finishing out his senior year. During my first year away from home, he acted as a protector and a surrogate parent to me. He was available to me to provide guidance and help me navigate my new existence. He provided me lots of space to explore and encouraged my development to find my own identity. He was part of the reason I decided to go to the University of Iowa—I wanted to be close to family.

During my senior year of high school, I successfully completed my applications to get into colleges but wasn't aware that I needed to complete a second application for housing. When I finally figured it out and submitted my housing application, I was put on a waitlist because all of the dorm housing was already taken. This was common at the time, because the University Iowa was a popular Big Ten school for people throughout the Midwest and particularly the Chicago suburbs.

When I arrived for my first day of freshman year, I was forced to share a study lounge that was converted into dormitory-style living quarters at the end of the eighth floor of a 12-story tower. While I was adjusting to being on my own as an independent adult, I was living in temporary housing. There were ten freshman boys sharing "the lounge"—five bunk beds in a room about the size of my parents' living room. The entry to the lounge was in the middle of the room and three bunk beds were on the left side of the room and two bunk beds were on the right. While I had shared rooms my entire life with my brothers and sister, I had never shared a room with nine people. I was the last person to arrive, so I ended up with the bunk bed next to the door with two bunk beds on either side of me. There was the constant noise of people arriving home and getting ready for bed. There were the alarm clocks and other noises that made it virtually impossible to get a good night's sleep. On top of the audio disruptions, there were the bodily smells of all of the sweaty, stinking guys. The room was filthy and smelled like a sewer.

In addition to all of this, there were personality and cultural differences. There were a couple of kids who grew up on farms and had been working the cornfields since they were barely able to walk and there were a couple of guys who grew up in Wilmette, Illinois, a tony suburb on the North Shore of Chicago who had never set foot in a cornfield. My bunkmate, Paul, the son of a Caterpillar engineer from Peoria, Illinois, and I had a few things in common, such as coming from large Catholic families. We quickly became allies and friends. Every night, someone came home stumbling drunk or one of the guys stayed in the dorm to smoke pot and get high. There was also a great divide between the guys who wanted to join fraternities and the guys who wanted to smoke pot. We named the groups—the "stoners" and the "frat boys." Paul and I were literally on the dividing line between the stoners and the frat boys, with our bunk bed in the middle of the room.

One example of the animosity that took place with the warring factions happened on a football weekend. One of the frat boys invited a childhood buddy to visit for the weekend. They went out to the bars and drank way too much. When they arrived back at the lounge, the guy puked his guts out all over the stoners' side of the room, pissing them off. The next morning, when the guy left to get something to cure his hangover, they threw his suitcase out the window and played dumb. Later that day, a fight erupted between the factions and Paul and I tried to calm them both down.

Paul and I did not take sides with either of these groups, so we were like Switzerland, acting as a neutral party with fighting factions all around us. The skills I had learned in junior high and high school came in handy as I could get along with both sides of the lounge.

The first two months were intense. Everyone was there almost every day and there wasn't an ounce of extra space. Gradually, some of the frat boys pledged fraternities and moved into their fraternity houses. The rest of us were waiting until someone dropped out of college and a vacant dorm room became available. Little by little, guys started moving out of the lounge and things became saner. I was one of the last ones left when a dorm room finally opened up for me in November, a couple of weeks before Thanksgiving break. I moved into a dorm called Quadrangle, a smaller, two-story brick building that was filled with sophomores and juniors, including several basketball and football players. Paul and I ended up sharing a room at Quadrangle. It felt like we had moved into the Ritz Carlton after three months of torture in the lounge.

My first semester turned into a nightmare and it was a very difficult adjustment. I wasn't sleeping a lot and was having a hard time adjusting to the harsh realities of the lounge life. I started to see a school counselor to figure out my feelings and manage stress. This was the beginning of my lifelong journey into self-help and therapy. My time with this counselor focused on the acute problems of the lounge and I didn't delve into the deeper issues of my identity. When I moved into a dorm room and my life normalized, I stopped seeing the counselor. The deeper issues I was avoiding would pop up again later and I would eventually start long-term therapy to resolve these issues.

While I grew into my own identity and started to establish myself as an independent adult, I continued to want to create a sense of family and connection with others. After moving out of the lounge, I felt a gap in my life. While I disliked the chaos and conflict of the lounge life, it was familiar to me and reminded me of my family life. When I was living with one roommate in the dorm, I didn't feel a connection to a larger group. While I didn't closely identify with the frat boys in the lounge, I did not identify with the stoners at all. Their laid back, chill mentality was contrary to everything that I had been raised to believe. I liked all the guys individually, but I did not approve of smoking pot. During the second semester of my freshman year, I decided to explore fraternity life through pledge week. At the end of pledge week, I decided to join Phi Delta Theta fraternity. The allure of a built-in community of brothers made me excited about joining.

After my first year of college, my brother graduated and moved to the West Coast. Besides my brother, I had a first cousin who was in Iowa City. I spent a lot of time with him as a child because we lived very close to each other and our mothers were best friends. I felt close to him and a sense of security knowing he was living in town. After my brother moved away, my relationship with my cousin grew closer. With my cousin and fraternity brothers, I created bonds that felt familiar with a sense of belonging, connection, and security.

As part of joining a fraternity, it was mandatory to live in the fraternity house for one year. I was not excited about this requirement. I knew that

I wanted to study abroad for a year, so I quickly moved into the fraternity house, which turned out to be very painful and a defining moment in my life. I ended up sharing a room with two fraternity brothers. One was my pledge father, Tom, and the other roommate, Dave, was the pledge son of my pledge father from another class. The room we shared in the fraternity house was small and our beds were located in a sleeping alcove in an attic above our room, which was accessible with a pull-out ladder. It felt like I had stepped back into the lounge style of living.

When I went away to college, I was conscious of wanting to be around a more diverse group of people and I had a clear sense of my values. Yet, I had not formed a clear political affiliation. The local government in our suburb did not have a very active role in the community. When I joined the fraternity, I was naive about the rivalries and values of the country's two major political parties. I wasn't a big fan of Ronald Reagan and his policies, but I hadn't voted in a national election and didn't have a political affiliation. After moving into the fraternity house, politics became front and center. When I joined the fraternity, I didn't realize that most of the guys—more than 90%—were Republicans. In the first semester of living in the house, there was an upcoming gubernatorial election. Terry Branstad, a conservative Republican who had been in office already and was a lifetime politician, was visiting our liberal public university for a series of events. My frat brothers invited Governor Branstad to the fraternity house for a meet and greet with the brothers.[3] I was disgusted with some of his policies and spoke up about wanting a fair and balanced approach to politics in the house. I requested that we bring in the Democratic candidate and they all refused. I called my buddy, Bruce, who was a reporter at the college newspaper and he covered the event as my guest, to the shock and surprise of my frat brothers. We were at least able to shine some light on this "campaign" appearance, though it was not enough time for what would have likely been a protested event for a Republican who was booed

---

[3] Japsen, "Branstad."

for cutting education funding throughout his many years as Iowa governor. These days, Branstad is President Trump's ambassador to China and a key figure in the trade war that is hurting farmers back in his home state.

With my stated opposition to the Republican candidate, I quickly became the outsider in the house. In fact, one of my pretentious, rich fraternity brothers, Pete, from Wilmette, was so troubled by my progressive political views that, when I ran for the fraternity pledge master, he influenced other brothers to vote against me so I lost the election. After that failed election, I was not included in various activities and felt isolated. This experience helped me build on my integrity of being true to my beliefs and honed my skills of speaking my mind in the face of opposition. It also helped me to think deeply about my values and beliefs to become more aware of how I wanted to show up in the world. There were others Democrats in the fraternity and we came together in our community to extol our beliefs. I didn't get kicked out of the fraternity or leave on my own. I became part of the opposition. I was disenchanted with the fraternity and couldn't wait to leave for Spain for my study abroad program.

CHAPTER 5

EXPLORING EUROPE AND MY SEXUALITY

FOR MY JUNIOR year of college, I went to San Sebastian, Spain, to study abroad for a year. San Sebastian is a cosmopolitan city in the Basque region of northern Spain. I selected this study abroad program at the recommendation of my Spanish professor, Roslyn Frank. She had roots in the region and had done extensive research on the area. I wanted to go to this program because it was based in an oceanside village close to many other European countries.

The study abroad program was the first time in my life that I was completely away from my family for an extended period of time. It frightened me to be so far away from everything I knew, and it excited me to forge my own identity without the previous constraints. Before the advent of the internet, I spent many days writing long letters to my parents and my family, sharing with them my experiences, my fears, my hopes, my dreams, and what life was like in a different country.

It was during my year abroad that I felt the freedom to start to dabble into understanding my sexuality and my attraction to men. I felt safer to express this part of my identity that I repressed for so many years. I liked the fact that I was so far away from home and I could avoid running into anyone I knew. It was in this space that I started to explore attractions to men. While living in San Sebastian, I never acted on any of my desires but became more conscious of them and started the long road to acceptance.

While living in Spain, I had a close-knit group of American friends: Bob from Boise, Idaho, was a gentle giant who towered over the Spaniards; Kelly from Redlands, California, was a nerdy blonde looking for romance, and Wendy from a wealthy family from Lexington, Kentucky, didn't have a care in the world except to have fun. Shortly after arriving in San Sebastian, my new American friends and I went to the discos for drinking and dancing. During this night of partying, a local guy named Tomas introduced himself while I was getting a drink. I had never been approached by a strange man in a bar before, and it felt like he was flirting with me. He was interested in practicing his English and looking for friends outside of his clique. We became fast friends and he introduced me to his network of close friends. With this group of new friends, my Spanish improved greatly. While Tomas wanted to practice his English, his friends only spoke Spanish with me. To this day, I am still very fluent in Spanish because of this complete immersion in the language.

Through these various friendships I started to understand more about human sexuality beyond heterosexuality. One night, Wendy took me to a bar with gay and bisexual people. This outing was the first time that I entered a space with openly LGBTQ people. I recall feeling very excited with the flirting and the idea that men could be attracted to me. It felt secretive and lewd to finally explore something about myself that I had always hidden or ignored. I didn't act on any of these feelings, but I was starting to confront my desires.

During my year abroad, I ventured to Ireland for the Christmas and New Year holiday. Once there, I stayed with extended family. These blood relatives treated me with kindness, respect, and love, even though they were strangers. Again, family made me feel safe and connected.

While traveling to Ireland, I met a French man in his early twenties named Francois. We spent several hours flirting on a train traveling from Paris to Calais. Francois had a slight build and an infectious smile and was very engaging. I felt excitement that I had never felt before. I was scared of these feelings and I was aroused by the sexual energy and attraction I felt toward Francois.

I had sex with women in high school and in college, lost my virginity to my senior prom date before heading off to college, and had short flings with two very attractive and sought-after women in college. During these encounters, I never felt emotionally connected and couldn't wait until they were over. I got turned on by having sex with these women and I liked the physical connection, but I didn't feel any attachment to them. I was acting and putting on a front.

I didn't speak French and Francois didn't speak English. I used some of my Spanish and a French translation book to communicate with him. I am not sure how we understood each other, but there was strong chemistry between us during the trip to the English Channel. At the end of the train journey, as we parted ways, he gave me his phone number and address in Paris.

When I returned to Paris after the Christmas holiday, I called Francois and went to see him. He lived in a small apartment with his cousin who was at work when I arrived. We sat on his couch for a few minutes trying to verbally communicate with each other through our different languages. There was incredible tension in the air. I felt his eyes lock on my face and body. There were words coming out of our mouths, but there was another form of communication happening between our bodies. Quickly, our hands started to explore each other. We fondled each other for a while and then undressed. We spent the next hour in each other's arms. Afterward, I took a shower and left. This was my first sexual encounter with a man. I felt alive like I had never felt before, but I also felt shame, fear, and self-loathing.

After this encounter, I immediately went to Notre Dame Cathedral and prayed for my sins. I went to confession and asked the priest for absolution.

I prayed ten Hail Mary's and five Our Fathers at the request of the priest. I felt so much remorse for acting on my desires. The lack of visibility or awareness in my community and the poor media representation of homosexuality had taught me that it was an abomination and wrong. I had transgressed against God and my family. I took those outside messages onto myself and turned my disgust inward. After this encounter, I felt so much self-hatred and I didn't want it to happen again. While I enjoyed having sex with Francois, I told myself that this experience was something that had to stay in Europe. In my head and body, I tried to push this away as an aberration. I had just shared sex and intimacy with a man, but refused to believe it was part of my identity. I fed myself this message to accept what had happened.

After finishing my year in San Sebastian, I traveled across Europe for almost three months. This journey was a time of tremendous growth for me. I explored new cities and met lots of people from all over. I stayed in youth hostels and slept under the stars when I couldn't find accommodations. I went for days without showering and relied on the most basic shelter. I mastered the rail and transit systems of many countries. I learned to communicate in many different cultures using English, Spanish, and many translation guides (this was all before technology like Google Translate). I interacted with people from varying cultures and connected with them through our shared humanity. I visited churches, museums, and endless cafes. I set aside a small pot of money for my travels and found ways to ration my spending to make it last for as long as I could. I traveled on a shoestring budget and did many things that I couldn't imagine doing today.

Initially, I left Spain and traveled all the way through France, Italy, and the former Yugoslavia to get to Athens. I spent time in both Athens and the Greek islands. I met some incredible people from the States, and we traveled around Greece together for a couple of weeks. I had a four-day romance with a woman from Georgia as I tried to forget about my rendezvous in Paris. With this brief affair, I was able to prove to myself that

I was genuinely straight and that the time with Francois in Paris was a fluke. I tried to push him and those feelings out of my mind and body.

After Greece, I went to Istanbul and spent a couple of weeks there. This excursion was my first time visiting a non-Christian culture, and I was surprised by the differences. When I arrived, I knew nothing about the Muslim world. Unbeknownst to me, I visited during the holy month of Ramadan. During Ramadan, Muslims are required to fast during the day and break the fast after sundown. After arriving, I remember eating in public and wondering why people were staring at me. After a couple of days, I figured it out. I had never visited a culture where men and women were segregated. I remember a group of Westerners from the hotel going to a bar. The group included one woman, and I didn't think anything about that until we arrived at the bar. She was the only woman in the entire bar, and I remember the Turkish men watching her every move. During my visit, I awoke to the call of prayer at 5 a.m. every day. The first day, it startled me, and I wasn't quite sure what was happening. I eventually got used to it, and it became part of my experience. My time in Istanbul challenged me to think differently about the world. My life experiences until that point had been very Western-oriented, and this adventure opened my eyes to another world of possibilities and people.

While in Istanbul, I became friends with a guy from California named Doug. He convinced me to hitchhike with him to Lake Ohrid in Macedonia. Lake Ohrid is located in the southwestern region of the former Yugoslavia and borders Greece and Albania. This portion of my travels was, by far, the most adventurous and dangerous. Doug and I became close during our week in Istanbul and were pretty much inseparable. While he told me he was straight, he acted differently from the guys I knew from the Midwest. He was soft, kind, and not obsessed with women. He was interested in experiencing different cultures and people and he was very open-minded. I felt attracted to him and questioned whether or not there was something else happening between us. I had tried to distance myself from my tryst in Paris and thought that something similar might be happening with Doug. I felt a struggle within myself to continue traveling with him because of these same-sex attractions coming up again, but I decided to go with the flow.

We left Istanbul, the bustling capital of Turkey, and hitchhiked to Lake Ohrid, over 400 miles away. I had never hitchhiked in my life, yet Doug convinced me it would be an adventure and easy to find people who would give us rides. We took a ride in a van that fit over ten people from the outskirts of Istanbul to the border of Macedonia. This interaction was the first time in my life when I came in contact with women who wore the burqa. It was a disorientating experience for me. I remember looking away and avoiding eye contact, which made me feel disappointed. I had always been taught to recognize everyone and, by looking away, I was not living by one of my core values. But I realized that I needed to respect the norms of the culture around me. Once we arrived at the border, we left the van and were forced to walk across since no one wanted to give rides to two Americans with all their belongings on their backs.

Once inside Macedonia, we struggled to get people to stop and pick us up for rides. In 1988, Macedonia was an incredibly poor region of Europe. While there were paved roads for the main thoroughfares, most side roads were dirt roads. There was no public transit system. The infrastructure was almost nonexistent. We waited at the side of the road in the middle of the night after one truck driver told us to get out of his van. We were forced to sleep in a ditch next to the highway until the sun came up. We returned to the highway to get a ride and waited for hours to be picked up. No one stopped to give us a ride. Finally, we lost our patience and stepped into the road to stop an approaching truck. We begged the driver to let us in his cabin, and he eventually relented. Once inside the truck, the driver tried to get Doug to give him his watch. He wanted to be paid for the ride and we found a few Yugoslavian dinar to give him.

Once we finally arrived at Lake Ohrid, we stayed for several days. A remote part of Yugoslavia, it was an incredibly impoverished place, and there weren't many Westerners going there. The stores' shelves were empty and people had almost nothing. We read a guide book about a great restaurant overlooking the lake. We went there for dinner and, when we tried to order, they didn't have most items on the menu. Everything we requested, they told us they didn't have. Finally, we asked what they did have, and the waitress responded with two items. So, we ordered and ate dinner. While we took in the beauty of the lake and the surroundings, it still felt desolate and depressing. I recall people staring at us all the time. I was very uncomfortable there and couldn't wait to get away. It was during this visit that I quickly became aware of my privilege as a Westerner and an American. When living in Spain, I came across people in modest circumstances in a few places, but never poverty. This village in Macedonia taught me gratitude for all the opportunities in my life. Afterward, Doug and I parted ways. He wanted to continue to explore the country and I had seen enough.

After spending over a week in the former Yugoslavia, I traveled to Budapest, Hungary. During my time in Istanbul, I heard from other travelers that Budapest was a beautiful, historic city like Paris but without the expense and crowds. It was still governed by the Communists and was off the beaten path of most Western travelers. It sounded intriguing and unexplored. My mother connected me with a family friend with relatives there. I took a night train from Skopje, Yugoslavia, to Budapest, which was about 500 miles away. I had a Eurail pass, which allowed for unlimited travel for two months. I had taken the night train a few times already and was able to get a good night's sleep. Unlike most of my travels in Western Europe, when I boarded the train from Skopje, there were very few passengers. I was able to find a cabin with accommodations for six passengers and had the entire cabin to myself. After eating dinner in the dining car, I returned to my cabin for a good night's sleep. I was able to stretch out and sleep across three seats.

I fell asleep easily and was in and out of sleep throughout the night. I awoke abruptly to someone touching me—a man was stroking my penis through my pants. He was in his twenties with pale skin, dark hair, and an average build. At that moment, I realized that he was wearing a train conductor's uniform. There was no one else in the cabin, and I was startled and scared. I was very disoriented when I first awoke and didn't realize what was happening. Once I came to my senses, I pushed his hand away and started to tell him to stop touching me. Of course, he didn't understand my English but he must have sensed my gestures. I was terrified. My mind was racing. What could he do to me? Was he a police officer? Could he arrest me? Who would believe me? After pushing his hand away, he walked to the door of the cabin and took his keys out to lock the door. He smirked at me as he was trying to lock the door and gestured toward his mouth. I looked into his eyes and I saw evil. I feared that he wanted to rape me. I felt this intense rush of adrenaline through my body and quickly jumped up and ran toward the door to stop him. I freaked out and started screaming at the top of my lungs. My screaming scared him away as other passengers began to come out of their cabins to find out what was happening. A woman in the cabin next to mine came out and stood there looking at me quietly like I was crazy and didn't do anything to come to my aid. A few others came out of their cabins with blank faces and didn't try to help me. By this time, the train conductor had disappeared. I was shaken and felt totally alone. I didn't know what to do or where to get help. I looked out the window and could see that we were no longer in the countryside and were approaching Budapest. I looked at my watch to see the time. It was 6:45 a.m. and we were due to arrive at 7:30 a.m. I had another 45 minutes before I could get away from that evil man.

I ran to the bathroom to pee and hide. I stayed there with the door locked for some time. Then, I realized all my belongings and passport were in my backpack in the cabin. I returned to my cabin to wait for our final destination. I was frantic. I was pacing. I was scared. I kept nervously looking at my watch to see how much longer it would be. It felt like the time stood still.

When I returned to my cabin to gather my belongings, the other passengers had returned to their cabins. Just when I thought I was out of danger, the train conductor returned to my cabin and approached me again. He gestured toward his groin and tried to get close to me. I screamed again. This time people came out quickly and he scurried off. I grabbed my bags and stood in the aisle waiting for our arrival in Budapest. I wanted to watch for him while being around other people and where I could run if needed.

When I got off the train, I felt vulnerable, exposed, and ashamed. Once I arrived at the home of the family friend in Budapest, I was in shock and felt disgusted. My host did not speak English and I did not speak Hungarian. She was kind and provided nice accommodations, but there was no communication between us. Over the next several days, I fell into a deep depression as shame washed over me. I believed that my rendezvous in Paris and my sexual attraction to men had been the cause of this assault. I felt that it was my fault. I played the incident over and over in my head. I asked myself what I could have done differently. What had I done to draw his attention? Was I stupid to think I could travel alone in Europe? Did I bring this upon myself? Were the sins of my same-sex attractions the reason for this assault? I walked around Budapest for the next few days in a fog. I went to see museums and explore the city, but I couldn't get the assault out of my head. It followed me around that city, and I was cautious about every person I saw. I was looking for the train conductor's face in the people around me. I was frightened that I might see him again and that he might assault me again. I was afraid that no one would help me.

This assault had a profound impact on me and made me feel worse about my underlying same-sex attractions. It pushed me further back into the closet and made me feel more ashamed about my sexuality and my identity as a gay man. It had happened while being away from my home and family, so I had a fundamental belief that my independence from family closeness and exploration of my attraction to men was part of the reason for the assault. I struggled to delineate between my identity and what happened to me. I felt I was somehow partly responsible. Perhaps this exploration of my sexual orientation led me away from my family and brought this unfortunate experience upon me.

I continued to travel through Europe, but I lost my sense of curiosity and excitement. It was replaced with shame, depression, and a loss of innocence.

I returned from Europe on my 21st birthday to celebrate the legal drinking age in America. But this rite of passage was something I'd been doing for over a year, so it was quite anticlimactic and seemed somewhat silly. After that summer, I went back to college to continue my senior year. I jumped back into my studies, my work, and my fraternity, which kept me incredibly busy. I tried to stay away from my feelings of attraction to men, and I did pretty well at it for a while.

Throughout this time, my family was always in my heart and my mind. I knew I wanted to have my own family someday. I didn't know how, when, or with whom. As I struggled with my identity as a gay man, I realized that I wanted to be a family man. I wanted to raise children and I wanted to create the unconditional love of a family. At this time, it felt like a binary choice—either a heterosexual family or gay individuality.

In the spring of 1989, my senior year of college, I started to study at a cafe in the heart of Iowa City. I found myself sitting there doing homework while looking around at bohemians, writers, and political activists, unlike my other friends who were in fraternities or into the bar scene. There was also a hidden sexual vibe that was new to me, and I felt the glances at me that I hadn't felt or hadn't been aware of before. I knew that I liked it and was excited by it. I was also scared when I realized that this energy was coming from men and that these feelings kept popping up for me.

At that cafe, I met an employee named Bill who I started to spend time with casually. Bill was the polar opposite of me. He was skinny and wore large-rimmed glasses that covered half of his face. He rarely smiled and was very mellow. He was studying English literature and was very introspective. He was involved in progressive politics and his group of friends were intellectuals. He didn't go to the sports bars to drink but instead went to poetry readings and house parties with friends. We had very little in common except that we were both from the north suburbs of Chicago. He grew up in Waukegan, which was close to the border of Wisconsin and on the shores of Lake Michigan. He once told me that he knew he liked men when he was still in his crib. His parents were divorced and his mother was an alcoholic. He had a difficult childhood and, unlike me, he was not close to his family at all.

At first, we became friendly with each other. We had so little in common and didn't have any interest in the same activities that it didn't seem like we could be friends. We spent a lot of time talking about our families, how we grew up, how we lived, how we wanted to live, and the things that were important to us. This man had piercing blue eyes, and I found myself drawn to him in a big way. As we spent more time together, I found myself looking for him on campus. Where did he study? What was he doing? How could we interact coincidently? While he seemed like he wasn't interested in me, it turns out he had been looking for me on campus, too. I started to want to see him more frequently and, when I didn't see him, I missed him. When I was around him, I felt peaceful and connected. It felt really natural to be with him. This was new for me. I had never felt this way with women or men before. While dating women, I always felt a need to be someone different than myself. In my previous interaction with Francois, I felt excited and turned on, but didn't completely feel like myself either. This feeling with Bill was different and special. I loved being around him.

Finally, on a Friday night, I had been out drinking heavily with some friends at a local dance club. I told my friends that I was heading home and stumbled out of the bar. The alcohol had removed all inhibition and the logical thinking that had been holding me back from acting on my attractions toward Bill. He lived in downtown Iowa City close to all the bars, in an apartment above a store. I rang the bell and asked him if I could talk to him. He let me in his apartment and asked me what I was doing there. He hadn't been out and was completely sober. He told me that his roommate was asleep and asked me to keep it down. I told him that I was too drunk to walk to my apartment halfway across town. He said I could stay until I sobered up. We started talking and then we started kissing. I started touching him all over his body and I started to undress. He kept telling me to be quiet. I wanted to have sex with him that night. After making out for a while, he told me to leave. He said that he didn't want to have sex with me while I was drunk. When he asked me to leave, I became combative. I had finally mustered the courage to explore my feelings with him and he was rebuffing me. I felt so ashamed, confused, and angry.

That evening was the first time that I kissed a man who I liked beyond physical attraction. I wanted to explore a sexual and romantic relationship with him. The next day, I woke up hungover and was in great despair. It felt like there was a shift happening and I was losing control over these feelings that were changing inside of me. It was like Pandora had opened a box and released my attractions to men and my sexuality. I was not going to be able to go back to the way I had been before. I told myself repeatedly that I would allow myself to have just this one affair before I would go back to my home, back to family, and start to lead a heterosexual life. I rationalized with myself that this was a one-time event and the last hurrah before starting life as a college-educated adult. Little did I know that my affair with Bill was the beginning of the long road to fully accepting my homosexuality.

After graduating from college in 1989, I moved back to my parents' home. I started to put my head down and, when I was working, I tried not to think about my attraction to men. I was trying to lead a very straight and narrow life. My first month back, I was really struggling with the loss of my relationship with Bill and my growing attraction to men. I couldn't fall asleep and once I fell asleep, I woke up often. I felt anxious, scared, and desperate. My mother took me to see our primary care doctor and, during my examination, I told him that I thought I might be gay and that I was having lots of difficult emotions. He recommended that I see a psychiatrist who might be able to help me. I became more worried. Was there something intrinsically wrong with me that needed psychiatric attention? Were these feelings irreversible? Would a psychiatrist recommend a drastic intervention? I scheduled the appointment with the psychiatrist for the earliest date, which was several weeks away. My mind was racing with lots of dark thoughts.

I started working at Dehaan and Richter Law Firm in the Chicago Loop as a law clerk. I had aspirations of becoming a lawyer and this clerkship was the first step. Every morning, I got on the train and avoided looking at men. I literally put my head down and stared at the floor. I hoped and prayed that these feelings would dissipate. When I looked up and saw an attractive man, I felt my heart jump, followed by a knot in the pit of my stomach. I told myself over and over, "Stop looking at him, you can control these feelings." I felt that I was losing control over my attractions to men and I wanted to control those feelings. I kept hearing the terrible messages about homosexuals being deviants, pedophiles, and predators. Was this my future? Were these things true of me? If they were true, I couldn't live my life this way. I needed to take action to stop these feelings before I did something terrible and I became one of those heinous people. I started to wonder what I should do if the psychiatrist couldn't help me. I started to think about taking drastic action and ending my life. I didn't want to die, but I wanted to make these feelings stop and I didn't know how to control them. I was terrified that I would be abandoned by my family and friends. I was terrified that I would become an outcast of society. I was terrified that I would never have a family of my own.

I talked to a couple of friends about killing myself. They pleaded with me to get help. It was 1989—before the internet, so there was very little public information about homosexuality and there weren't LGBTQ centers nearby. Everything was underground. Even compassionate friends just didn't know that much about being gay and didn't have resources to share. I didn't want to meet other gay people because I didn't want to experience attractions and I didn't want to associate with them. I felt very lonely and isolated. I drank heavily to escape my feelings.

A few weeks after joining the law firm, one of my coworkers, Lori, invited me out for a drink, and we met one of her friends. Chris was a gay man living an out and proud life as an artist and AIDS activist. This period was during the heart of the AIDS epidemic and Chris was unapologetic about his lifestyle and politics. I found myself excited about meeting Chris, but I was scared about socializing with a gay man so close to home. I was afraid that my colleagues and friends would see us socializing and wonder if I was gay, too.

Finally, I had my appointment with the psychiatrist. I remember very little about the doctor. I was nervous to see him and find out what was wrong with me. When we started the appointment, he went through my medical chart and started to ask basic questions. I didn't tell him I was thinking about suicide. I knew that would create a red flag and cause a swift reaction. He was clinical, professional, and detached. He was neither empathetic nor uncaring. He simply gathered information about what was going on with me and stated facts about homosexuality. While the psychiatrist never said homosexuality was normal, he said that a small percentage of people were homosexual. He didn't make me feel it was either good or bad. He recommended that I start taking medication that would help me with my anxiety and put me to sleep. I don't recall what drugs he prescribed but I didn't want to start taking them. After hearing the unbiased information about homosexuality, I decided that I didn't want to dull my feelings with medication and that I needed to deal with these feelings head-on. I was still depressed and anxious but I knew that there were other people in the world who were also gay.

With the information from the psychiatrist and my acquaintance with Chris, I slowly started to feel less self-hatred and my mood started to improve slightly. I came out to my parents as being bisexual or gay. I wasn't firm about these identities yet and was trying to gauge their acceptance. My father cried, which was difficult to watch. My mother said that it might be a phase. She said she knew of other family friends who had questioned their sexuality but eventually, they realized they were straight. She didn't cry and seemed nonchalant about it. She told me that even if I was gay, it was important for me to eat my dinner. They both affirmed their love and commitment to me regardless of my sexual orientation. They said we should keep talking about it and they were interested in making sure I felt supported.

During my high school years, I was part of a close-knit group of friends who did everything together. They had been the center of my world. During my college years, we stayed in close contact and whenever we returned home, our relationships resumed where they left off. I started to come out to a few of these close friends and, in general, it was a positive experience. They mostly expressed their love and commitment to me. But, while no one disowned me or expressed outright hatred, most of these friends didn't know how to relate to me or connect with me as a bisexual or gay man. I felt distanced from them, but I couldn't figure out if it was related to us preparing for the next phase of life post-college or if they were uncomfortable with my sexual orientation.

While I felt a sense of relief and support from my parents and friends, I continued to lie to my parents about where I was spending time outside of work. I often told them that I was going out with my high school friends and then met Chris and Lori for drinks and bar hopping. During one of those evenings, I went to this really trendy bar called Berlin near the Belmont L station. That evening, I met a man named Dan and we started to date. Dan was Irish American and four years older than me. He was tall, muscular, and had wavy blond hair. He was very handsome and very sweet. He was the youngest of seven children. He had finished high school and started college but never finished. Dan was working as a heater and air conditioning repairman in the western suburb of Chicago, Downers Grove. He had grown up in an affluent family and had been provided everything he wanted. He dreamed about moving to Hollywood and becoming an actor. His mom lived close by and, whenever he had money issues, she would give him a "loan." He was completely comfortable in his identity as a gay man and was hoping to meet another gay man for a relationship.

While Dan was a well-adjusted, honest, and kind man who wanted to date and have a long-term relationship, this was the farthest thing from my mind. I was hiding my relationship from everyone and lying to my parents about where I was spending my time. I couldn't be honest with myself and I couldn't be honest with them. I didn't think I would ever have a family. I still felt like I had to make a choice between having a relationship with a man or leading a heterosexual life with a wife and children. I never conceived that I could have it all. I finally couldn't hide the relationship with Dan from my parents any longer. While we were out to dinner on a Saturday evening, I told my parents that I had been seeing Dan for the last four months. It was a very heated discussion about this relationship, this man, and my lying. While we hadn't talked about my identity over the last several months, I never told them that I was acting on my attractions and having sex with men. They were surprised and unhappy about this revelation. I think that they had hoped that my bi or gay identity would go away or that it was truly a phase. Their positive response eight months prior had given me license to go further into my exploration of my sexuality. But for them, the lack of discussion meant it wasn't important to me. Shortly after the contentious conversation, I left for California.

PART 2

COMING OUT

CHAPTER 6

IDENTITY CRISIS

M Y OLDEST BROTHER, Bill, was living in northern California in San Ramon, a Bay Area suburb of San Francisco. He called and invited me to come to visit for the summer. This excursion was a great way to run away from my budding relationship with Dan and get away from my family and friends. I felt shame, fear, and a lack of control over these attractions.

I left my parents' home in May of 1990 at 22 years old. I drove a 1975 Saab coupe that my parents' next-door neighbor, Ras, gave to me for the adventure. Ras was an eccentric man who grew up in northern California and attended Berkeley in the 1960s. He encouraged me to leave the suburbs of Chicago and explore the West. I planned to move to California for the summer of 1990. I was trying to escape from my past and what was happening inside of me. Summer turned into fall, fall turned into winter, winter turned into spring, and spring into summer again. And that cycle kept on for about five years. I kept creating excuses to avoid returning home. I was too ashamed to ask for what I needed to be happy. I was terrified of being alone for the rest of my life. I was terrified of losing everyone that I loved. I was terrified of losing the life I knew. I was terrified of the unknown.

When I started to come out, there were few images of queer people in media and public life and were almost no positive images of gay people. During the 1980s, I remember hiding to watch episodes of the TV sitcom *Soap* with Billy Crystal's character as a gay man. I loved watching the show, but it scared me because people hated his character due to his homosexuality. In 1985, Rock Hudson died of AIDS. He had been completely in the closet and, even on his deathbed, never acknowledged his homosexuality. His death was the stuff for supermarket tabloids and led the front page of the *National Enquirer* for days. During Ronald Reagan's presidency, Reagan refused to utter the acronym AIDS. Today, the death of a celebrity with AIDS fuels national movements and marshals people to a cause, whether it's AIDS research or support for civil rights. The message that I got from all the reporting on Rock Hudson's death was that lying and hiding were necessary for me.

While it had been five years since Rock Hudson died, things hadn't changed much. This was during the first term of George Herbert Walker Bush's presidency. The Republicans were fighting AIDS drug research and there was great hostility and fear toward gay people. This political climate and the shame and secrecy of being queer made me afraid of the future of living my life as a gay man.

During my first summer in California in 1990, I worked as a busboy at Charlie Brown's in San Ramon where my brother was the manager. I went out after work with the other employees, and we drank a lot. This is the typical behavior for many in the restaurant industry. After a long, busy night taking care of other people, we went out to drink, relax, and decompress. My drinking took on another purpose. I got intoxicated to numb myself from my attraction to men. I would expel so much energy trying to fit in and cover up my feelings. It was exhausting. Then, I would need an outlet for it, and I would drink to run away.

One evening, after finishing work and having multiple drinks, I was driving back to Bill's house and got pulled over by the police. I remember when the sirens went on and thinking that I was going to get arrested. I was sitting in my car, waiting for the police to arrive at the window. I told myself to get serious and fake sobriety. When the police asked me to get out of the car and walk a straight line, I did the best I could. I slowly walked on the line in front of the car and kept telling myself not to fall over. I did mostly well with some swerving off the line. I lied and told the officers that I wasn't drunk but nervous. They bought it, and I drove home very slowly. That was the last time I got drunk and drove. In the future, I would find other ways of getting around after a drunken binge.

In the fall of 1990, I decided to take a human sexuality course at the University of California, Berkeley. I knew almost nothing about this topic. I repressed my sexuality and had pushed down those feelings for most of my life. I ignored my body and attractions at all costs. I took this class to try to understand this new world that I was exploring. My classmates were open-minded and diverse in their backgrounds and ideologies. I started to forge new relationships with them. It opened my eyes to the world that I didn't know existed and it also made me very uncomfortable.

While taking this class, I decided to move to Berkeley. I had been living with Bill and his wife, Anne, for several months in a small two-bedroom townhouse in San Ramon. I had overstayed my welcome and Anne encouraged me to spread my wings and find a place of my own. I responded to an ad to rent a room with another person in North Berkeley in a rundown apartment. While I still hadn't decided to permanently live in California, I was looking for a cheap place to live. It was meant to be temporary because I kept thinking that I would return to Skokie.

In my first six months in California, I was making a conscious decision about my future. I thought about this decision like I had control over my attractions while deep down inside I knew that wasn't true. There are the two schools of thinking about homosexuality—nurture versus nature. For me, my attractions to men felt innate, much like the color of my eyes. I was making a conscious decision to lead a life of truth as a bi or gay man or a life of lies as a straight-acting family man. I could choose to continue to suppress my feelings and be with a woman and create a family. During college and high school, I had faked through those identities. But I was seeing a glimmer of another possible life as a gay man and trying to gather as much information as possible to make that decision.

As part of that discovery, I experienced bi and gay life in different settings. I took anonymous excursions into San Francisco to see and feel the vibe of the gay scene. During this time, I wasn't sexually active. I was continuing to try to push those feelings away. The other part of my discovery was through reading about other people's journey through self-acceptance and self-love. I read memoirs from gay authors. I read self-help books about finding a partner. I was terrified of making a decision to lead a life as a gay man and then being alone. I was searching for answers in these books and memoirs. I traveled to San Francisco alone or with Bill, and we would go to City Lights Bookstore in North Beach where I would go off into a corner and look for books about queer people.

During one of these visits I encountered a book titled *Quiet Fire: Memoirs of Older Gay Men*.[4] I wanted to understand what it would be like to be old and gay. I had no idea what this meant, as I knew no one who fit that profile. I wanted to hear their stories and understand how they were living their twilight years. I read this book with such intensity, focus, and hope. I was looking for clues about what my life might look like if I followed this path. I searched for answers that would allow me to say yes to being true to myself. I was looking for stories of love and normalcy and longevity and happiness.

The book described the unique lives of 17 gay men from many walks of life. It contained stories of wealthy single gay men who traveled the world, men with partners, men living alone, and one man living in a residential hotel on the brink of homelessness. The spectrum was vast and

---

[4] Vacha, *Quiet Fire*.

showed both happiness and sadness and everything in between. I read each word of this book with a view of the future. I was trying to imagine myself in these stories and how I would feel in my later years. I kept this book to myself and shared it with no one. It was the key to the future for me.

Reading that book was a turning point for me. It taught me that there was a way to move forward with this identity as a bi and gay man. There were no guarantees of what the future would hold but there were many possibilities. I remember thinking to myself over and over that if I was going to lead a life as a single gay man without a family that I wanted to be affluent. I wanted to take care of myself, travel the world, and find comfort in a variety of cultures. I made a conscious decision to work hard, and that gave me support in accepting this path for my future.

I started to venture into San Francisco more frequently to experience the gay night life. After work on a Wednesday evening, I went to the gay bar called The Stud, which was one of the oldest gay bars on the West Coast—it had opened in 1966. Wednesday night was a busy night with lots of men in their early twenties like me. I met Paul, from a French Canadian family, who had grown up in the suburb of Fremont about 30 miles away from where I was living in Berkeley. When Paul and I met, he told me that he was 21 and finishing up college. He lived at home with his mom and siblings. He came out when he was 14 and was very comfortable with himself. His parents were divorced and his mom was an alcoholic. His brother had been incarcerated for getting into fights and drinking. About two months after we started dating, he told me that he was 19 years old and he had entered The Stud with a fake ID. This did not go over well with me. He lied to me and it took him over two months to be honest with me. I kept wondering what else he was keeping from me.

When I eventually got over his dishonesty, we started spending more time together and got more serious about dating. I had just moved to the area and didn't know anyone. I liked dating Paul because he was an insider to the Bay Area and had experience in the gay community. He helped introduce me to gay life without having to do it on my own. I mostly liked spending time with him but I wasn't in love with him. I slept over at his family home at least once a week and interacted with his dysfunctional family. We shared a small, single bed where he slept with his head on one end and I slept with my head on the other end. In many ways, our relationship felt like a close friendship with sex. While his family life was chaotic, he showed me that there was a way to live openly as a gay person and get the love from family and friends. Even though he was younger than me, he was a great teacher about self-esteem, self-love, and self-acceptance. He accepted himself and didn't care about the outside world. We dated for about six months and then we started to have some problems with schedules and priorities. He was going to community college and working. I was working nights and weekends in the restaurant industry. He had very little time for a relationship and I was struggling with my self-identity. We slowly drifted apart and the relationship fizzled out.

As our relationship ended, I started to feel less in control of my feelings and fell apart emotionally. I started to see a therapist to help me understand what was happening inside. When I started therapy in 1991, my goal was to stop feeling so much and try to be more even keeled. I felt things very deeply and being in a relationship with Paul made me realize that some other men didn't seem to feel as much or didn't share those feelings. I wanted to emulate them. I wanted to feel fewer emotions, especially melancholy and loss. I wanted to be detached from my emotions. I started seeing a therapist, who—to this day—I still see.

After moving to California, I had started to come out to my siblings. I came out to Bill and Anne and then came out to Bob and Julie. They all expressed their love and support for me, yet there wasn't a lot of openness about the topic of my sexual orientation. I think it made them uncomfortable and they didn't want to talk about it openly. To help bring more understanding for them and allow them the space to understand on their terms, I sent each of my siblings a copy of the book, *Now That You Know: A Parents'*

Guide to Understanding Their Gay and Lesbian Children. I had read this book to help me understand what it might be like for my parents and siblings dealing with my coming out. My parents and I started to have more open conversations about my sexual orientation. After sending the book to my siblings, I never heard from them that they received it or read it. From their silence, I figured out that they weren't comfortable discussing this area of my life. In many ways, I wasn't comfortable with myself yet, so how could I expect them to be? Despite their unwillingness to discuss my sexual orientation, I was resilient in knowing my truth and trusting in the underlying strength of our relationships.

When Bill transferred back to Southern California for his job, I faced a difficult decision to stay in the Bay Area without my brother or move back to Chicago to be near my immediate family. Every time I spoke with my parents, they asked me when I was coming home. I always responded soon, or I replied when I complete such and such thing I'll go back. For five years, I never bought a bed and I was always planning to return to Illinois.

After Bill moved away, I was living on my own in Northern California. I was forging a new life for myself. While I knew my family and friends loved me, and I wasn't disowned for being bisexual or gay, we rarely discussed my life as a single gay man. Most of my relationships with my high school friends became nonexistent. Eugene, Tom, and I stopped talking and I saw them periodically during visits back to Skokie, but the closeness and intimacy were gone. I pulled away from them because I feared rejection and they were starting to get serious with girlfriends and jobs. I spent time with my family frequently, but the topic of my sexual orientation was rarely discussed.

When I think back on this time of my life, I can see how sad and lost I was. In many ways, I lost my family and my friends. I felt lonely and I was alone. I was very determined to figure out who I was, what my values were, and how I wanted to create my life. This time in my life, I did not have a lot of responsibilities and could explore relationships and the world as I wanted. This period was a time of incredible growth, self-work, and exploration. With each new adventure, I had faith in myself. I had faith that each experience would bring me to new learning, which would ultimately lead me to the next encounter. Starting in the fifth grade and through my youth, I learned the valuable lesson of resilience and picking myself up when I was down.

I was exploring my new identity as a gay man. I was grieving the loss of identity of a straight man, a family man, a Catholic man. I spent a lot of time thinking about my desire to be true to my attractions and identity, and how that road might be more difficult and isolating. I thought a lot about not having a family of my own. I thought a lot about the choice between a relationship with a man and having a family. Added to this was the fact that it was also during the AIDS epidemic and gay men were dying all over the Bay Area and the world. The choice between a heterosexual life with family, safety, and health seemed much more appealing than a life full of loneliness, loss, and death. In so many ways, it felt like the wrong choice to live as a gay man, but I couldn't keep up the facade any longer.

CHAPTER 7

THE IMPACT OF
THE AIDS EPIDEMIC

A FTER MY RELATIONSHIP with Paul ended, I decided to lead a slightly more open life as a gay man. While deep down inside, I knew I was gay, I often told people I was bi because it was more acceptable. After coming out to myself and then my direct family, there was the process of coming out to extended family, friends, coworkers, and others I encountered every day. This process of coming out would last a lifetime as I encountered new people who viewed the world through a heterosexual lens.

During this transition to my new identity, there was a lot of confusion, discomfort, and awkwardness. I struggled because I didn't have the skills or experiences to interact with other men. Through my high school and college years, I had been putting on a mask to show up for dates with women. It never felt natural to me, but I observed my friends and learned from them how to show up to interact with women. I mostly faked it through those years. I learned how to ask women out and show interest. I even learned how to have sex with women, but it wasn't authentic. It felt pleasurable to be with women, but it made me feel nervous during these interactions and empty afterward. I could be the man who others wanted me to be, yet I wasn't living my true identity.

When I finally started being myself and explored relationships with men, I felt like a child. I didn't know how to interact and behave with men. I was excited and attracted to men yet felt utterly inadequate in pursuing meaningful relationships with them. When I came out to myself, I was born into a new identity and starting from square one in finding myself and finding love. When I was in elementary school, junior high, and high school, I experienced my first same-sex attractions, I denied them and pushed them away. During these formative years, I did not have my first experiences of flirting, crushes, and initiating romantic connections with others. I avoided interactions with girls because I wasn't interested and I avoided interactions with boys because I was in the closet. Even though I was 23 years old, I felt and acted like a child.

During this time, I was thinking about the desire to have a family of my own. While I moved very far away from my biological family, I was still very connected to them in many ways. I had created a family of choice, and I was building strong platonic relationships along the way. Meaningful relationships and human connections were the fundamentals of my personality and drove me personally and professionally. My desire to have a family of my own continued to pop up along the way, and I longed to meet someone to share this dream. As I was meeting men and dating, I was always checking into whether or not they were interested in having a family. Some were vehemently against it, and that made the decision about dating them easier. Others were less certain about wanting a family. For many gay men, their experience with family was painful due to their sexuality and feeling disconnected from their families. I struggled to figure out which men were uninterested in having a family and which men might want a family but were uncertain due to painful experiences. I always relied on my faith in God to guide me. I prayed that God created me in his image, and I was perfect in God's eyes. This faith in God gave me comfort in my hours of loneliness. Because I believed God had a plan for me, I found a meaningful connection in my life when it was meant to be and when I was truly ready.

In Spring of 1991, my living situation in Berkeley deteriorated. My roommate, Mike, had lied about how he was using my rent money and I found out that Mike had been swindling me. Mike tried to tell me another story about how he was using the rent money, which was another lie, and when I confronted him, he became defensive. He moved out shortly afterward. I stayed in the apartment for a couple more months and then moved to Oakland with a coworker, Kevin, who was one of my first gay friends.

Kevin was a really funny and sweet guy. He grew up in Omaha, Nebraska. He was the only child of a Mexican-American Army man who served in Asia where he met Kevin's mom, a Japanese woman, during his tour of duty. Kevin was a Buddhist and very devout. I was immediately enthralled with his background and his faith in Buddhism. Kevin had a difficult time growing up in the Midwest with his diverse background and being gay. He came out to himself at 13 years old and struggled to belong in Omaha. Kevin and I were both waiters at Skates on the Bay in Berkeley. We went out after work often and became close friends. When his living situation changed, we decided to look for an apartment together. We found a great two-bedroom spacious apartment close to Lake Merritt in Oakland.

Shortly after moving to Oakland, I started to notice two men living together in an apartment across the street. I noticed one of the men seemed quite ill and the other man was helping him get up and down the stairs. This went on for a couple of months. Eventually, I met one of the men whose name was Michael. He was a skinny, Caucasian man with hollow cheeks. He was funny and very sweet. We slowly started to talk to each other as we were getting in and out of our cars, unloading groceries. After a while, I stopped seeing the other man and saw Michael on his own. I was curious what happened but didn't want to pry. He eventually invited me into his apartment for a drink and he shared that his partner had passed away from AIDS. I was shocked and scared. It was the early 1990s, and there was so much disinformation about AIDS. While I knew that AIDS could only be transmitted through the exchange of bodily fluids, it scared me that I could somehow contract HIV/AIDS. While I was sexually active at the time, I was always practicing safe sex and was very careful about the type of sex I was having. In those days, safe sex meant using a condom for any sexual activity. Shortly after I started spending time with Michael, he informed me that he too had AIDS. He was on medication and was feeling mostly well. When his partner died, he left him an inheritance and Michael was using the money to take care of himself and trying to do all the things he had never been able to do as a young man.

Over the next year, Michael and I became good friends. I wasn't fully out and was very careful about who I told I was gay. I was dating and having sex in the midst of the epidemic, which made sex scary and risky for me. It felt like such a dichotomy: having sex made me feel so good and alive, yet unprotected sex was killing people. The AIDS epidemic made me very distrustful. While I wanted to engage in relationships and sex with men, it also made me afraid of contracting HIV. During this time, there was so much ignorance and fear. Whenever I spoke with my mother, at the end of almost every call she said, "Be careful and I'll pray for you." While she was never explicit in what she was praying for and what I should be careful about, it always felt like she was telling me not to get AIDS. I eventually asked her to stop saying that at the end of our calls.

Over time, Michael and I became closer and Michael became more ill. He was losing weight and getting sick more often. On a couple of occasions, he got pneumonia and was bedridden. I helped Michael by bringing groceries when he wasn't able to get out of his house. Over time, Michael shared his story with me. He grew up in Wisconsin and was rejected by his religious family for being gay. They disowned him and he moved to San Francisco to live as a gay man. He came to the city with nothing and started to work as a prostitute to make money. He used drugs during his hustling to lower his inhibitions with strangers. With the AIDS epidemic, everyone was supposed to use condoms. Some of his customers paid him more to have sex without a condom. Many of these customers were older and had never used condoms for sex and they didn't want to use condoms despite the ongoing epidemic. After contracting AIDS, Michael met his partner who also had AIDS. He stopped hustling and using drugs. He got a regular job and they eventually became a couple. Their mutual HIV status allowed them to experience each other fully without worrying about contracting AIDS.

In 1992, Michael became progressively worse. He had a close friend, Jim, who moved into his apartment to help take care of him. A few months after Jim moved in, Michael got sick again, but this time it was worse. He became bedridden. Jim was providing him around-the-clock care. As Michael got more ill, we spent more time together. I came to his apartment to sit and read to him because his vision was going. When Michael knew he was getting worse, he begged his father to come and see him one last time. His father told him some story about not being able to buy a ticket last minute on a Friday and he needed to wait until Monday. Michael was very disappointed that he wouldn't see his father that weekend. After speaking with his father on Friday evening, he worsened. On Saturday afternoon, I came to see Michael and Jim before heading out to work. While Jim and I were holding Michael's hands on either side of the bed, visualizing a meadow of beautiful flowers with a house in the distance, we told Michael we loved him and that his partner was waiting for him in that house. Michael took his last breath and he died. I was stunned. We sat there for a while and wept. This was the first time that I had witnessed death firsthand. We cried and we felt relief for the end of Michael's suffering.

After Michael died, I was heartbroken for a long time. He had experienced so much rejection, pain, and loss. I wondered if I would experience those things from my family and friends if I got AIDS. I felt proud that I was HIV-negative and I felt guilty about being proud of it while others were HIV-positive. It was a complicated time for HIV-positive and HIV-negative men to be in relationships and date. During this time, there was so much shame and fear of gay men and even more for HIV-positive men. I wondered if AIDS and death would happen to me for living my truth. Michael's journey, suffering, and death made me want to live a long, hopeful life as a gay man. I didn't want to end up as Michael had.

On April 25, 1993, I attended the March on Washington for Lesbian, Gay, and Bi Equal Rights and Liberation.[5] I went to Washington with a group of friends from California. The march was a rallying call for LGBTQ people to show the world that we existed everywhere and that our lives mattered. The march was planned during the Bush presidency, when his administration was pushing policies and laws that attempted to silence the LGBTQ community. The March on Washington was a watershed moment for me. It was a huge celebration of LGBTQ people from all over the country. Over one million people from different ethnicities and backgrounds, young and old, black and white, gay and straight, came to Washington to demand equality. It felt like something so much bigger than myself, and my experience was shared by millions. It gave me a sense of pride, confidence, and purpose. As part of the march, the AIDS Memorial Quilt was on display and I found the patch of quilt that had been sewn together in memory of Michael. The display of the quilt was a solemn reminder that, while there was a need for celebration, there was also pain, suffering, and loss.

After spending several days in Washington, DC, I left for New York City to experience gay life on the East Coast. While San Francisco was bustling with the gay rights movement, it felt like a small town and not a big city. I was intrigued in visiting NYC to expand my experiences as a gay man. I went to the Village and the Stonewall Inn where the modern gay rights movement was born in 1969. One of my best friends, Jill, who I met when we worked as waiters together for several years at Skates on the Bay in Berkeley, grew up in New York and had many friends still living there. She connected me with one of her oldest friends, David, who lived in the

---

[5] Schmalz, "March."

Village with his partner. David opened his beautiful home to me for ten days while I explored NYC.

During my time there, I met a handsome Japanese man named Takashi. Takashi was from Tokyo and was a classically trained pianist studying in NYC. Takashi was kind and demur, with beautiful brown eyes and gelled hair that stood straight up off his head. He was tall, elegant, and composed. He was the polar opposite of me. I didn't have a musical bone in my body. His hands and musical talent were his gifts. In fact, he had $1 million of insurance to protect his hands from injuries. I was a waiter and working hard to make a living. Takashi was into the good life and he introduced me to fine dining, the theater, and the arts in NYC.

After our initial time together, Takashi and I began a long-distance romance. Every two to three months when he had a break from school, he came to Oakland and we cohabitated, or I went to NYC. We hung out during the days and, while I was working at the restaurant at night, he went to Japantown or Hotel Nikko in San Francisco. Takashi was never very interested in sex. He mostly liked cuddling and foreplay. I think this served me well because I was still trying to figure out how to be sexual amid the AIDS epidemic. I enjoyed the intensity of the relationship for a couple of weeks and then the break when he left. I definitely wanted a relationship but was too inexperienced and immature to actually have one. We dated for about one and a half years. I went to Tokyo with him to meet his family and we took several vacations together. During one vacation to Hawaii, we had an intense argument about our philosophies on life and I ended up sleeping on the bathroom floor. He didn't understand or like my desire to live an open, honest life as a gay man. He was closeted and wanted me to be closeted, too. Eventually, he was planning to return to Tokyo to get married and live a closeted life like many Japanese queers at the time. During our long-distance relationship, we were monogamous. During his last visit, I told him that I wanted to date other men during our time apart. He became outraged and pushed me against the wall. He called me a whore and held me against the wall for several seconds while he spewed his anger toward me. I told him to take his hands off of me and get out of my apartment. I refused to be in an abusive relationship and be shamed into something that wasn't true. I had my own demons about my identity but was unwilling to take his shame and self-hatred onto myself. While we made up after this fight, this was the last time I saw him.

In 1995, I finally met someone with whom I shared a powerful connection. On a Thursday evening, while I was out dancing at The Box, a gay dance club in the South of Market neighborhood of San Francisco, I noticed a man dancing on a platform in front of the club. He had long brown hair in a ponytail and a lean, muscular body. His shirt was off and he was wearing leather shorts and boots. He was stunning and he turned me on. I was attracted to his face and body and his bravery, confidence, and aloofness. While I watched him dance, he hardly noticed me. He was in his own world, enjoying himself and largely ignoring everyone around him. I watched him for a while and finally caught his eye. When he eventually took a break and came down off the platform, we started to talk. His name was Rocco and he lived in San Francisco. We talked for a few minutes and then agreed to talk more after he finished dancing.

We had similar backgrounds in how we were brought up and our close relationships with our families. We were very different in many other ways, but we shared the same fundamentals of values, respect, and kindness. There was a connection on a profound level, and our bond grew quickly. From the outset, we were spending a lot of time together, and there was a real potential for a long-term relationship.

After six months, Rocco wanted to move in with me. I felt strongly that the relationship was still in its infancy and we needed to endure the test of time and tension before cohabitating. Call me old fashioned, but I had a rule of two years of dating before living together. My gut told me that the honeymoon of the relationship was not the reality of a long-term relationship. I believe that arguments and strong disagreements test how we handle differences and they provide insight into how the other person reacts or deals with the conflicts. During our first six months together, we didn't have big disagreements or fights and I still didn't know how we would recover when we had one. I also wanted to continue to have autonomy and an identity of my own.

While we shared many important qualities, we had stark differences in how we lived our lives on a day-to-day basis. I worked as a restaurateur in San Francisco and I had a very unorthodox schedule. I started my shifts in the late afternoon and I was responsible for closing the restaurant after everyone went home, sometime between 11 p.m. and 3 a.m. By the time I got home and was able to fall asleep, it was usually after 2 a.m. While most people were relaxing and connecting, I was working. Rocco was a freelance architect and an incredible artist. His artwork was the center of his life. When he was engaged in an art project, everything else fell out of focus, and he had little time to engage with me or anyone else. Rocco was much more introverted than me and preferred to spend his time alone. For me, when I was not working, I liked to spend time with friends and create relationships. These differences caused me concern about our connection, but also made me think about how we would manage a family. At that time, we were probably too young to start a family but would these behaviors change if we ever decided to? Then there was the aspect of practicality. He was a big dreamer and didn't believe in taking traditional steps to achieve a dream. He could live on a shoestring budget and didn't consider in savings for the future. He lived in the present and threw caution to the wind. I admired this quality in him but I was always thinking about the future and planning to achieve my next goal. For Rocco, everything revolved around his artwork from a time, resources, and focus perspective.

During our relationship, we took a trip to the Midwest to meet my parents and siblings and to attend a friend's wedding. I had left Skokie five years earlier, this was the first time that I was bringing a boyfriend home and coming out to a broader group of people. I was anxious about my family and friends liking him and Rocco liking my family and friends. Rocco and I had been dating for about a year and were committed to each other. We didn't stay at my parents' house because they forbid unmarried couples to share a bed in their house. Since gay marriage wasn't legal, it wasn't an option for us. I felt sad that our relationship didn't get the recognition of a married couple but I respected my parents' rules. We ended up staying at a hotel in the city and commuting back and forth to spend time with my family. It turned out to be the best thing in the end because it allowed us more time to explore Chicago and spend time together. The trip went mostly well, but the cracks in what we wanted from a relationship started to become more apparent. He liked meeting my family but didn't envision a life where we visited family often. His family lived in Hawaii and he spoke with them often but didn't vacation with them.

A few months later, we received an invitation to my cousin's wedding in France and he didn't want to come. He said he didn't have the money for the trip. When I offered to pay, he said he wasn't interested in meeting the extended family and he didn't like weddings. My cousins were a big part of my life growing up and I loved going to these wedding because they were like family reunions. I was sad about his decision but decided to go without him. The wedding was amazing. I took an extended vacation with my sister, her fiancé, and my parents. We spent time in Paris and Burgundy. It was an incredible trip.

When I returned, there was a gap between us. While I was away, we tried to talk on the phone a couple of times but, with the time change and different schedules, we only spoke once. The time apart gave Rocco the space to focus on his artwork without interruption. He didn't want to go back to the way we had been relating to each other. He wanted more space and less commitment to focus on this artwork. While I was away, he had injured himself and didn't go to the doctor to take care of it. When I found out, I was surprised and very concerned that he was fully recovered. He got angry for asking questions about his decisions about his health care and inserting myself into these matters. I had the belief that couples were responsible for each other, and part of that responsibility was taking care of each other's health. I was hurt and angry that he felt I shouldn't share this part of his life. After this disagreement and the time apart, we broke up.

I was devastated by the breakup. Over the next year, I felt lost without him. We had grown so close and we were practically living together. I missed him desperately. While I knew it was the best decision in the long term, I was one step further away from starting a family. I had taken two steps forward in having this meaningful, connected relationship where I learned so much about myself and what I was looking for in a long-term relationship. After the breakup, I had taken a huge step backward and was back to square one, trying to find a partner before starting a family.

Seven years had passed since I came out, and I finally realized that there was a pattern in the men that I was dating. I was attracted to strong, emotionless men who made me feel safe. I liked their strength and stoicism because I felt vulnerable and emotional. I kept meeting and dating men who were emotionally unavailable to me. While I liked their self-control, I wanted a deeper and more profound connection. I tried to change them into being more emotional and connected, but this proved fruitless. While I enjoyed the physical connections and the cat and mouse game of flirting and dating, I was no further along in the process of finding love than when I first came out.

In 1998, I started working for Wolfgang Puck at Postrio, one of the most highly regarded restaurants in San Francisco. It was a dream job for a restaurateur. I was the assistant general manager and sommelier. I dove into my job and was working very long hours. I was meeting celebrities such as Jacques Pépin, Julia Child, Keanu Reeves, Tobey Maguire, and Newt Gingrich and I was even lucky enough to serve President Bill Clinton during the height of the Monica Lewinsky scandal. I was having success at work and making a name for myself in the close-knit San Francisco restaurant scene. I put my dating life on the back burner.

Over the next five years, I dated periodically. There was the excitement of the possibility of a connection and long-term relationship. In some cases, when the relationship ended, I was relieved because there was no real connection and I was trying hard to make the relationship work. In other cases, there was sorrow over the loss of the relationship. Through each experience, I learned more about what I wanted from another man and what I couldn't handle in a relationship. While I continued to learn and grow, I became weary, cynical, and skeptical that I could find love. I wanted both a partner and children. As each relationship ended, I felt further away from the hope of finding true love. I started to contemplate what it would be like to be a single parent. I felt conflicted about giving up on finding true love.

Throughout all of these dating challenges, I continued to dream about having my own family. I continued to be very involved with my biological family and my family of choice. I became the godparent to three of my nieces and nephews. I celebrated the growth of my siblings' families through weddings, birthdays, baptisms, and all the other family celebrations. I lived vicariously through them. I celebrated their milestones as if they were my own because I never knew if I would have my own family. This closeness with families made me feel wistful on the one hand because I always felt like I was looking from the outside. On the other hand, it gave me a glimpse into the intimacy of their relationships and motivated me, even more, to make this happen for myself. When a relationship failed, I would grieve the loss, then pick myself and try again. I said to myself repeatedly, "You have to kiss a lot of frogs before meeting Prince Charming." This saying would give me hope amid loss.

CHAPTER 8

FINDING TRUE LOVE

I N AUGUST 2001, I had a new career as a sales representative for a pharmaceutical company. I dreamed about starting a family and began to think more seriously about doing it on my own. I was sure I wanted to be a parent, and the clock was ticking, but I felt uncertain about doing it alone. I also felt like I wanted to parent with someone who I loved and with whom I could share both the joys as well as hardships along the way. I had become very lonely and longed for love.

Professionally, I was feeling good about my accomplishments. I had been very successful in meeting my sales goals and been recognized with awards and sales incentive trips. I was now working a routine schedule of Monday through Friday during standard business hours. In my previous life as a restaurateur, it was challenging to have meaningful relationships because so many of the men I was meeting had more traditional sched- ules. I had grown tired of dating and I was itching to do something for myself. I trained for a half marathon for the Gay Games (Gay Olympics) in November 2002. It was great to have a goal and focus on myself. It built up my confidence and made me feel good about myself. I went to the Gay Games with a new friend, Jeff. We met through a mutual friend six months earlier and we instantly connected. We went to Sydney with a large group of people and Jeff and I shared a room together. Jeff was swimming in the Gay Games and I was running a half marathon. Jeff and I planned a two-and-a-half-week trip to Australia. While in Sydney, we spent a lot of time exploring the city, attending various sporting events, and getting to know each other better. After Sydney, we spent a week in the Great Barrier Reef and Australian Rainforest. Our friendship grew during those two and a half weeks as roommates.

On Superbowl Sunday in January 26, 2003, Jeff and I went to a fund-raiser at the Eagle Bar in the South of Market neighborhood of San Francisco. The Eagle is a well-known leather bar that also hosts outdoor beer busts on Sundays for local charities. Jeff's swim team had overspent their budget for the Gay Games and was raising additional funds at the beer bust to cover their expenses. I went with Jeff, not expecting to meet anyone. While most Americans were glued to their TVs watching the Superbowl, I met my future husband in a random encounter.

Jeff and I spent a lot of time hanging out during the fundraiser. After a while, we went our separate ways to chat with other people. When I first saw my future husband, his back was to me, and I could hear his infectious laugh. I couldn't see his face. He was about the same height as me. He was wearing cargo shorts, a T-shirt, a baseball cap, and running shoes. The cap was pulled over his face in such a way that it was hard to see the profile of his face and his eyes weren't visible. He had brown, slightly hairy legs. His calves were bulging. His shoulders were wide and he looked like he was very fit. He was very animated, and I could see from the people around him that he was very engaging and that everyone was under his spell. I observed him for a while before getting a chance to see his face. I knew from this laugh and the aura that came from his personality that I wanted to meet him. I decided to say hello and tapped him on the shoulder. When he turned around and I saw his face for the first time, I was in awe. Not only did he have this mesmerizing energy, but he was drop-dead gorgeous.

He had a beautiful smile with brown eyes, hair, and skin. He appeared to be Asian or Pacific Islander. He was smiling ear to ear and laughing. We looked into each other's eyes and my heart skipped a beat. For me, it was immediate attraction and desire. I had never really experienced love at first sight, but this connection felt like that.

We introduced ourselves and had a casual conversation while he was there with a group of friends. He introduced himself as Lori and I introduced myself as Steve. When he said his name was Lori, I was confused. He was this strong, handsome man with a woman's name. It didn't make sense to me. I asked him how he spelled it and he said "L-O-R-I." He explained to me that it was abbreviated for his full name, which was Lorevic and that most people could never pronounce his full name correctly, so he shortened his name to avoid educating people. He went on to explain that his full name was a combination of his parents' names, Loretto and Victoria. Lore + Vic = Lorevic. I thought wow—what a great name! How did I end up with such a boring name like Steve? I loved the way his name sounded. While his friends called him Lori, I never called him by that name. From that day forward, he was Lorevic to me.

We chatted for a long time at the fundraiser, flirting and getting to know each other. There was a strong mutual attraction. After a few drinks, his friends wanted to go to the Lone Star, a half a block away, and he invited me along with the group. I didn't want to let him slip away, so I followed him there. Shortly after we entered the bar and got a drink, I took his hand and asked him to go on a tour of the bar with me. He was incredulous and wondered where I was taking him. This was my first time in the bar and I hardly knew where I was headed but I knew that I wanted to break away from the group and get some alone time with him. While his friends were all nice, I had spent enough time with them already and wanted to get this handsome man alone. We walked around the bar for a minute and then I spotted the outdoor beer garden. While we were chatting under the stars, I reached over and kissed him for the first time. It was magical. His lips were like pillows from heaven. I had awoken from a long sleep. I felt alive in a way that I had never felt before. I never wanted that kiss to stop.

As the night wound down, I found out that Lorevic was in a relationship with another man. They had recently broken up after four years of dating and were in the process of trying to work things out. I was disappointed but not surprised because some men in San Francisco were in open relationships. I had tried an open relationship with a married man once before but it didn't work out for me. It was clear to me that my old-fashioned Catholic upbringing wouldn't allow me to be in an open relationship, so I considered this evening with Lorevic was a romantic tryst and nothing more.

At the end of our first night together, I turned around after we parted ways and thought to myself, I could fall in love with this handsome, captivating man. I knew he was still involved with someone else and that I would be heartbroken if I tried to navigate a relationship with him. I felt a deep sense of sadness that I had met this amazing man and he was not available to me. I also felt great happiness because feeling that connection and desire gave me hope again about finding love and fulfilling my dreams of being in love and a relationship.

After we parted ways, he kept creeping back into my mind, and I pushed him away. I didn't want to long for a man who was unavailable or partly available. I wanted a man who was fully available for me and a relationship with me. Fortunately, a few weeks later, we ran into each other again. I had stopped on Castro Street to get cash at an ATM. He happened to be walking down the street and we literally ran into each other. Our connection felt stronger and more intense during this encounter.

We continued to have these casual encounters at bars and coffee shops. During these interactions, we flirted with each other, and I continued to fall in love with him. I wanted us to fall in love from a place of independence and desire. I had entered relationships in the past from the place of dependence and need, and I was grateful that I had learned these lessons. Finally, one day, we went to lunch to have burritos. It was during this lunch that we started to talk more about our dreams and future. I remember asking him what things made him tick and what was most important to him. He was in the process of finishing his undergraduate degree, and he was dancing professionally. He aspired to do his best and succeed in whatever career he chose. He wanted to be in a loving relationship and someday, in the distant future, have children. When he asked me the same questions, I remember stating definitively that my family and friends were the centers of my world. And creating lasting connections with people was paramount to my life.

After this lunch date, we went back to my apartment and I told him about my feelings toward him. He was on his way to San Diego for a weekend partying and drinking with his friends. He told me that he and his boyfriend had broken up but that he wanted to spend some time single before dating anyone. I told him that I agreed, and it was probably good for him to have some space to process the relationship. I said to him, "When you love someone, you have to let them go." I wasn't sure what I was saying. I just knew that he needed to grow and develop on his own and come into a relationship with me from a place of desire and not from a place of rebound. At that time in my life, I desperately wanted a partner, and I don't know why I made that statement. It surprised me, yet my past experiences had taught me that trying to bring someone into a relationship who wasn't ready for it was a losing proposition.

Shortly after he returned from San Diego, we started to date, and rapidly our relationship became serious. I had been single for quite some time and was hesitant to commit. I didn't want to jump into things so quickly. I struggled with really trusting another man. He, on the other hand, wanted me to commit to being exclusive with him and not date other people. I said no, and we agreed to continue dating. For me, I had fear around jumping into things too quickly and getting attached to him to face the potential loss of a breakup. I was also very aware that we were in very different places in our lives. I was in the process of starting my MBA program and he was finishing his undergraduate degree. I wanted to start a family after my MBA was complete, and he was just getting started in his career.

The decision to continue dating other men turned out to be meaningless because when I had free time, I only wanted to be with Lorevic. He brought me so much joy, excitement, and love that I only wanted to be with him. It was during this courtship that we went out to dinner and a movie one night. When he dropped me off at my condo, I blurted out to him, "I love you." I hadn't planned on saying it. I had tried not to say it because I wanted to protect myself from another potential breakup. After about five months, we became exclusive and fully committed to each other. We were a couple and we were seeing each other whenever we had time. A few months later, we went on our first trip together to NYC and had an incredible time.

Over the next couple of years, we each pursued our personal goals for education and careers. We worked on our relationship. We took lots of trips together and we began to combine our groups of friends. Everything was moving in the right direction, and I felt thrilled that I had finally found someone to love and someone to love me. In the back of my mind, I was still thinking about creating our family. We were also spending time with our respective families, and our ties to each other were becoming more interwoven with each other's families. It was becoming clear that we were in this for the long term.

After about two years, we decided to move in together and make the next commitment to each other. I was living alone in a one-bedroom condo on the edge of South of Market and he was living with a roommate in a small two-bedroom apartment in Noe Valley. Neither of us had a space big enough for both of us, so we embarked on buying a home together. It was 2005, at the height of the housing market boom, so we couldn't afford anything in San Francisco and decided to look across the bay in Oakland. This decision was a massive step in our commitment to each other and our relationship. It also involved our respective families because we needed help with the down payment, and they stepped forward to help us. I remember feeling so happy that both of our parents wanted us to buy a house together and wanted our relationship to succeed. This step was a real turning point in my identity as a gay man. First, I was finally involved in relationship with a man who wanted more commitment with me. Second, I felt another level of acceptance and support from our families that I never imagined was possible. During times of turmoil in our relationship, I have relied on my family to help me through those difficulties. I think that many queer people lack the support of family to help them when there are challenges in their relationships. I know it has been a tremendous help for me.

After spending some time looking at various properties in Oakland, we landed on a new townhouse development of 90 homes in West Oakland, close to the Bay Bridge and two freeways. While we wanted to buy that townhouse, it wasn't that easy. The housing market was so hot and there was such a shortage of affordable housing that we were forced into competing in a lottery system for the townhouse. During the previous night's sleep, I dreamed that we won the lottery and got our first choice. Early on a Sunday morning in the summer of 2005, Lorevic and I went to a park across the street from the development to get a number and wait for the drawing. There were about 100 people there and the chances of winning looked very slim. The lottery was the first phase of the release of ten homes. We were so excited about the townhouse and crossed our fingers. They turned the drum with all the numbers and the first number drawn was for an Asian couple from San Francisco. They turned the drum again and the second number drawn was our number. We jumped in joy and yelled, "We won!" They continued until ten numbers were drawn. While we didn't have first choice of our home, the first couple decided on a different floor plan and we were able to select our first choice. We were excited, but it was also comical that we entered a lottery to *get* a townhouse and a mortgage. Aren't lotteries supposed to work the other way—to help people *get rid of* their mortgage? Winning the lottery felt like a good omen about our future together. Everything was falling into place and the universe was behind us.

After we bought our first home together, I was ready to take the next step in our relationship to have children. This desire started to bring tension in our relationship. Lorevic and I are eight years apart in age and we were in different places in our lives. He was starting his career in the business world after a very successful career as a dancer. I was on my second career and was beginning to feel like my clock was ticking. Both my brothers started their families in their early twenties and their kids were leaving home for college. My sister's children were under ten, and I wanted our kids to have cousins around their age. My parents were getting older, and I wanted to share my children with them. After buying a house, I felt more financially settled and not as worried about being able to provide for children. The other thing that was a constant reminder was the fact that we couldn't just decide to have children and get pregnant. We needed to rely on others outside our relationship, whether through a surrogate or adoption. Either route would require significant planning and time, which was starting to feel pressing to me.

Lorevic wanted to focus on his new career to become an expert. He was also interested in traveling and having fun with colleagues and friends. We were at a bit of a standoff for a while. In pursuit of his dreams, we started traveling more frequently and made a habit of taking a big international trip every other year for Christmas and another trip during the year. We hosted dinner parties and birthdays and had fun. I kept pressing Lorevic on his desire for a family. He told me over and over, he wanted children but not yet. I was growing increasingly frustrated and finally, during one of our vacations, we had a series of conversations to figure out why he was not ready yet. He wanted to pursue his MBA before starting a family and he felt that once we had children that it would be impossible to complete his graduate work. I had completed my MBA and knew how much it meant to me. I wanted him to pursue this goal, so we developed a compromise. He would quickly start his MBA and after he completed the program, we would start our family.

He entered a 21-month MBA program while he was working, and for the first few months, we hardly saw each other. The program required a total immersion, and he was in school on weekends and study groups during the weeknights. It was a lonely time for me as I was so ready to take the plunge to start a family. I had achieved a certain level of success at work and had a great deal of autonomy in my day-to-day work environment. I was ready for the kiddos and yet had to continue to wait. He progressed through the program and did well. After the program, we start to move forward with exploring the options.

I recall us having so many conversations about having kids related to the timing of our careers and how we would manage our careers and family. One of us was always either in a new position, a new company, or both. There was never a good time to start a family. We were still conscious of one of us slowing down in our career for some time to be available during the critical junctures of development for our children. For an impatient man like myself, it took too long.

The journey to become a parent was so fraught with factors outside of my control—finding love, finding a partner who wanted to be a parent, finding someone with similar personal and professional goals, and finding someone who also valued family over everything else. It was a very long road from first coming out years earlier to this point of starting a family. All of my dreams were coming to fruition. It wasn't happening on my timeline, which taught me essential lessons—acceptance, persistence, resilience, kindness, love, and letting go of factors outside my control. While I was learning these lessons, I didn't fully understand how they would help me in the long term. All of these lessons would serve me well in parenting.

PART 3

EXPLORING PARENTING

CHAPTER 9

SURROGACY OR ADOPTION?

FTER LOREVIC AND I finally got to the places in our lives where we were both ready to start a family, we needed to figure out how. How would we become parents? Since we are two men, there was no way for us to do it on our own. We thought a lot about what was important to us and then we needed to agree on those decisions.

Family formation was an area where neither of us had vast knowledge or expertise. We didn't personally know many LGBTQ people who had kids. We heard stories about local queer politicians and celebrities who were raising children. Many lesbians had children but far fewer gay men had children. There was Ricky Martin and Neil Patrick Harris and David Burtka, who had fame and fortune to create a family through surrogacy. At the time we started our journey, the surrogacy option seemed very expensive. It was a couple of years after the great recession and housing crisis. We were significantly underwater on our mortgage, and it looked costly to do surrogacy. On top of the expense, we had other considerations.

From an adoption perspective, we didn't know many gay dads who had adopted kids. There was Dan Savage and Terry Miller, who were role models for adoption. They chose a child from a homeless woman and Dan wrote about it in his book *The Kid*.[6] I felt especially inspired by Dan Savage and his partner since Dan, best known for his nationally syndicated sex column *Savage Love*, grew up in an Irish Catholic family in Chicago, which felt very similar to me. Neither my husband nor I had grown up with adoption in our lives. Before the 1980s, closed adoptions were the norm and parents didn't tell their children about their birth families. I had a friend in junior high who was adopted. I recall him finding out during junior high and how he was traumatized by the news. As an adult, I had one friend who had been adopted from Korea. He was adopted at six years old and talked about his experiences in the orphanage in Korea. My cousin and his wife were thinking about adoption after having two biological children. I recall a very uplifting conversation with his wife about adoption and her encouragement about LGBTQ adoptions. Other than these few stories, adoption was relatively foreign to both of us.

Neither of us had any real familiarity or attachment to either adoption or surrogacy. We spent a lot of time thinking about what family meant to us. As gay men, we had become familiar with the concept of a family of choice, which in many ways described how we related to our close friends. A family of choice is people who deliberately choose one another to play significant roles in each other's lives and take on many of the emotional parts of a family of origin. We both moved away from our biological families to discover our identities. I moved from Chicago to the Bay Area without any friends and almost no family. My husband moved from San Jose to San Francisco and lost communication with his family for some time. Independently, we both needed space to explore ourselves and our identities.

During these separations from our biological families, we created the lives of our own and families of choice. The first several years of living in California, I spent most of the holidays with my family of choice. My first family of choice included, Jill, who became one of my best friends, and another friend, Tom, who I met through a gay church group. We created traditions and memories together. With my family of choice, I no longer

---

[6] Savage, *The Kid*.

felt the strong need to connect to my biological family. When I did connect with them, it was out of love and desire and not out of obligation. While this was happening for me, I wasn't conscious that my concept of family was changing. I didn't realize my idea about what defines a family had transformed until I started to seriously consider creating my own family.

We started to talk about our family and asked ourselves questions about what constitutes a family and what was important to us.

As we thought about surrogacy, we asked ourselves all of these questions:

- Did genetics make a family?

- Did it matter to us if our children resemble us?

- Was it necessary to us that we knew the family health history? Did we think our genetics were so good that we wanted them to be carried on?

- What do blood and genetics mean to us?

- If we were going to create a genetic family through surrogacy, whose sperm would we use? Whose egg would we use?

- Would we ask one of our sisters for their eggs? How would their families/spouses feel about it? How would we share with our children their egg donor?

- How would we select an egg if our sisters said no? What would be essential to us?

- How many kids would we have?

- Did we want twins?

- How would one of us feel if the genetics were only from one partner?

- Who would carry our child? What would our relationship with the surrogate be?

As we considered adoption, we asked ourselves these questions:

- Would we be comfortable not knowing the genetic/medical history of our child?
- How would we explain the adoption of our child?
- What kind of adoption did we want? Domestic, foreign? Open adoption? Closed adoption?
- How would we feel about the uncertainty of adoption?
- How did we feel about race, gender, etc.?

As we thought about having a family, we gravitated toward adoption for many reasons. First, we believed a family was created through love. When I finally met my husband—"the one"—I knew that love was the most important and profound part of our relationship. It wasn't education, background, class, status, ethnicity, or genetics. It was love and connection. If we never had children, we were already a family that was not formed by blood relations but by love. So why should it be any different with our children?

We did not feel a firm attachment to our genetics. For me, I had two brothers and four nephews between them, and there was no need to carry on the family name or genetics of family. In Lorevic's case, he was the only son to his parents, so this presented more pressure on the genetic front, yet he didn't feel strongly connected to his genetics either.

Our first foray into adoption occurred in the summer of 2009. As we started to gather information, we looked at learning more through events hosted by local adoption agencies. We did a lot of reading online and we were interested in learning from adoption professionals. Lorevic and I were in a positive space about our sexual orientation. We were both entirely out to our families and at work. We lived authentically and engaged in open and honest relationships. As we were exploring our options, we wanted to work with an agency that was 100% comfortable and open with working with same-sex families. We decided to pursue a few different opportunities to gather information and figure out what we wanted. Over the next few months, we attended informational sessions at three different types of adoption agencies:

1) a domestic, open adoption agency,

2) a domestic and international adoption agency, and

3) a foster-to-adopt program through Alameda County Social Services Agency.

First, we attended a two-day information-gathering workshop hosted by an open adoption agency located in the Bay Area called Independent Adoption Center (IAC). We were attracted to this agency because many of their families were LGBTQ couples and singles. This agency hosted a two-day workshop and, initially, we were reluctant to spend so much time with strangers talking about something so intimate and private as starting a family. We wanted a one-hour info session with a somewhat anonymous atmosphere where we didn't have to share too much about ourselves. The agency didn't offer that type of workshop. We were forced to sign up for the two-day event, which, in hindsight, forced us to examine our commitment and family values.

The two-day workshop was inspiring. IAC employed one of the leading experts on open-adoption, Kathleen Silber. She had pioneered the concept of open adoption back in the 1980s when closed adoptions were the norm and she published research on the long-term benefits of open adoption.[7] An open adoption is a form of adoption in which the birth/biological parents make decisions about the placement of their child with an adoptive family and may continue to have contact after that. The ongoing contact with the

---

[7] Silber, *Children.*

birth family allows the child to understand their origins before their adoptive family placement.

In a closed adoption, the birth family and child do not know each other or do not have access to information about each other. The identities of the birth parents and child are concealed from each other. During this two-day workshop, we became very comfortable with the concept of openness and access. IAC explained that the childhood development of fantasies about birth families is very pervasive for adopted children. Understanding their origins either through information or meeting the birth family helped children with their identities. While this seemed more complicated for us to navigate, it seemed like the best thing in the long-term well-being of the child.

During this two-day workshop, we learned about the challenges of heterosexual couples who struggled with fertility. We knew about infertility and had a few acquaintances who went through in vitro fertilization (IVF). We were unaware of the emotional and relationship toll that infertility created for couples. We were surprised that many of these couples (primarily women) were so ashamed of their inability to get pregnant and there was a tremendous sense of sadness and loss about their infertility. In some cases, there was secrecy about their plight. One woman in the group who finally turned to adoption as a last-ditch effort for starting her family shared that she had been trying to get pregnant for over five years. She hadn't told anyone outside her husband about her infertility issues. She described going to family events where her parents and others would inquire about them starting a family, and she would not share their struggles.

This shame and hiding brought me back to my days of being in the closet. It reminded me of the time and energy I had spent concealing my identity and the lost opportunities of building deeper relationships with a shared experience. Her struggle with infertility and the stories of others in that workshop impacted me greatly. I felt lucky and relieved that our infertility issues were clearly understood based on our same-sex anatomy. We were relieved of the societal pressures of creating a family. In the 1990s and early 2000s, once you told people about being LGBTQ, the expectations about family were immediately dismissed. For us, starting a family was entirely on our desire. There were no expectations, and we could define it how we wanted to construct it for ourselves.

The experience of engaging with these heterosexual couples struggling with fertility reminded me of the normal bounds that bring humanity together. These couples were experiencing many of the same feelings that I had experienced as a gay man trying to figure out my identity. The shame and loss were universal. The circumstances and situations were unique, but the feelings that I had experienced were very similar to what these couples were experiencing. This experience allowed me to look at heterosexual couples differently. Previously, in my view of the world, I did not think that heterosexual couples faced significant hardships due to the privileges of being part of the mainstream culture. This experience shattered that view and gave me greater compassion and understanding for their challenges.

We liked the executive director, Anne, and many of the social workers at the open adoption agency we met during the workshop. We felt comfortable and connected to the agency, the other families that were pursuing adoption, and the mission of the agency. We felt like we belonged and the agency staff respected us as a couple. We felt a great sense of relief that we were not on our own anymore.

Next, we attended a two-hour information session with a domestic and international adoption agency in San Francisco called Adopt International. Adopt International is a private agency that did some private domestic adoptions and many international adoptions. It was a brief two-hour informational session. It provided great insights into their mission, yet lacked any feeling of the act of adoption or parenting. It felt very mechanical and detached.

Many of the couples attending the workshop were interested in adopting from China and Korea. For many in this group of prospective parents, their interests were in having closed adoptions where their adopted children would not have contact with the birth families. In the case of many foreign adoptions, there is a complete lack of information about birth parents and, where there is information, the international adoption agency holds it tightly. From all that we had learned about child psychology, adopted children spend a lot of their time wondering about their birth families. In some cases, worrying about the birth families and their well-being. In other instances, the adopted children fantasize about how their lives and families would be different and better with their biological families.

The benefit of foreign adoptions was the certainty of the legal status when you gained custody of the child. In foreign adoption, the adoptive parents leave the country of origin after completing all necessary paper-work and the adoption is finalized. For the waiting period, the children were often living in foster homes or orphanages while the paperwork was in process. This waiting period could be six to 12 months in the best of circumstances and many cases, up to two years. While the certainty of the legal status in foreign adoptions was alluring, we wanted a newborn and we wanted to be with the child as they developed from the beginning.

Lorevic was born in the Philippines, and we were interested in doing an adoption from there. We learned that the law required the adoptive family to live in the country for two to three years after taking custody of the child and before leaving the country with the child. We understood why, but it was not possible for us since we were both holding down busy jobs in California.

Even if we were willing to adjust our expectations to consider foreign adoption, most countries would not allow LGBTQ families to adopt. As the gay rights movement solidified protections for queer families in the United States, foreign countries started restricting international adoptions for LGBTQ couples. Currently, there are only two countries that allow same-sex couples to adopt—Brazil and Colombia.[8] When you review how many

---

[8] Considering Adoption, "LGBT."

foreign adoptions these countries are allowing, the chances of a child being placed in your care are almost impossible.

We walked away from this information session feeling disappointed and sad. Discrimination toward LGBTQ couples wanting to adopt was a reality both internationally and domestically. These restrictions for queer people adopting children reinforced a negative world view of LGBTQ people. On some level, it made us question whether or not we could be good parents? Was there something that all of the groups were saying that had some validity? Or was this the remnants of years of discrimination? Whatever the reasons behind this discrimination, our choices for creating our family were narrower than we had hoped.

Our final event was hosted by the East Bay Gay Men's group for the foster-to-adopt program through Alameda County. This event was completely different than the other two workshops in the fact that it was exclusively gay men and mostly Caucasian men. As we did our family formation research, we had primarily been interacting with straight couples. This event felt different in its energy, dynamics, and stories. The group was composed of a wide variety of men from different age groups, neighborhoods, and at various decision points in the journey to adoption.

The speaker was a social worker from Alameda County. She was an African American woman living and working in Oakland, and the contrast with the group of almost exclusively white men was stark. She led a very engaging discussion about the foster-to-adopt process. She explained the ins and outs of how you go from fostering to adoption through myriad complicated steps. For us, it was tough to understand what she was describing since we had such limited knowledge of the social services system. The discussion focused largely on the circumstance of how these children came into the foster system. She described situations of domestic violence and drug abuse. All of this was information that we had previously read or heard about, but this time, it felt different. As we were thinking about bringing a child into our family, this conversation made us face the circumstances that many people go through that we do not encounter. For me, this session made me vividly aware of the advantages we experienced in our jobs, education, and living situations. It made me think deeply about the potential trauma and suffering that a child might have experienced before coming into our lives and their ongoing challenges. All things from their past, well beyond our control, would become part of our lives. More importantly, it made me wonder if I had the skills and background to help a child with trauma overcome their previous experiences and flourish. This discussion upended my idealist view of love conquering all. It also made me think a lot about my upbringing and some of the bullying that I had endured. This reminder made me sad and made me think about a defenseless child and the adults bringing these children up in the world.

The social worker described the goal of the foster system for Alameda County is to reunite children with their birth families and to avoid placing children for adoption. This reality was another slap in the face. Our goal was adoption and having a child in our lives forever. We didn't want to take care of a child to have them returned to a family that had caused them harm. Fundamentally, this didn't make sense to me. My naive perception of adoption came crashing down. She described a process where the birth family is receiving services to rehabilitate themselves to take back their child and the foster parents are moving forward with an adoption plan. Adoption was a perfunctory choice if the birth parents failed to meet their goals for recovery. We had no idea that the foster system's intention was focused on reunification. We had been focused on adoption and had envisioned foster parenting as a mandatory step. This session opened our eyes to the reality of this system, and it scared us.

After this last session, we decided that we could not live with the uncertainty of the foster-to-adopt system for our first child, and we wanted more certainty in the process. We could not imagine bringing a child into our home with the hope of adopting that child only to have that child removed from us to return to their birth parents. Perhaps we were too selfish in our desire to become parents. More to the point, we could not imagine giving and receiving all the love of that relationship and bonding with a child who couldn't stay with us. It scared the hell out of us and made us think about our journey to become parents. Being a foster parent is a brave calling and requires a selfless person who can love, nurture, and grow a child without conditions of longevity. This session gave me so much respect and admiration for the people who take on this selfless duty. We were so determined to build our family; we couldn't make that decision at that time.

After this period of considering the choices for adoption, we landed on open, private adoption as the way to start our family. We were so excited about having a new addition to our family. With this vital decision behind us, we started working on the more mundane but equally important tasks of becoming adoptive parents. We chose IAC as our partner for creating our family. As part of the process, we needed to create a profile for birth families to learn more about us, which included a website and brochure. As part of the home study, we completed mounds of paperwork, background checks, a visit to our home, and other administrative hurdles. We were interviewed by social workers and attended classes. All of this work took about six months from beginning to end. When we started this process, we didn't realize that we were embarking on a marathon. We were so excited with our decision and couldn't wait to bring a child into our home. We failed to realize how long we would be waiting and how difficult the waiting would be on us.

CHAPTER 10

THE UPS AND DOWNS
OF ADOPTION

A FTER THE LONG and grueling process of getting approved to be adoptive parents, we were finally ready to meet birth parents. In April 2010, we were finally live on IAC website and our profile was open to prospective birth parents. At that time, two and a half years felt like the longest wait of our lives. That was how long we waited for our daughter. The National Adoption Center estimates the wait for a healthy baby is typically between two and seven years.[9] By those standards, two and a half years seems like a flash in the pan, but it's still a long time to put your life and dreams on hold.

Those first six months of preparation felt like a mad rush to get everything turned in. Once everything was submitted and we were listed, we thought we'd be flooded with calls. We expected the phone to be ringing off the hook the moment we got the green light. We were constantly checking our phones and making sure our 800 number was working and

---

[9] Adoption Center, "FAQs."

transferring calls to our cell phones. And we didn't get so much as a crank call that first month.

IAC had tried to set the right expectations to help us prepare for the wait that would ensue. There were at least 200 families ahead of us at our agency alone—all vying for that one child. But their advice went in one ear and out the other. All we cared about was matching with the birth parents and holding our bundle of joy. We were ready to be fathers. We were ready for the bottle feedings. We were ready for the diaper changes. We were ready for the sleepless nights. We wanted our child and we wanted it now.

Our placement social worker, Annie, gave us a false sense of hope in an off-the-cuff remark. She said something along the lines of "as a mixed-race, gay professional couple" she thought our wait would be shorter. The official agency advice was an average of 18 months of waiting prior to finding our child. Annie explained that many birth mothers placing children for adoption preferred a two-man household because the birth mothers did not feel like they were being replaced by another mother. She said a heterosexual couple made some birth mothers feel threatened. For a same-sex couple, it would become obvious to the child and others that there was a birth mother versus an adoptive heterosexual family with a new mother in her place. We thought there was finally an advantage to being gay.

In the months and years that followed, we were contacted by 14 different women in varying stages of pregnancy. Most were legitimate, while others felt like they were running scams or that their stories just didn't ring true. Yet, we took every phone call, email, and text that came through seriously, wondering if our future child and birth family were on the other side of the call. None of these contacts resulted in an actual live meeting.

Our first call was nerve-wracking. We were so nervous when we saw a number come through that we didn't recognize. We played hot potato with the phone, saying, "You take it!" "No, you take it!" "I don't know what to say!" IAC provided us with suggested questions and talking points to break the ice in these very awkward conversations. We had those questions pinned above our desks and role played how the call would go. Needless to say, all the preparation in the world never got us ready for that first call. We had dry periods where we were wondering if we'd ever be contacted again. There would be months where we wouldn't hear anything and other months where we were juggling two birth mothers at once.

By the way, sit down and talk with your partner about how you're going to address these contacts, what you're going to say, who's going to take the call (or email, text, etc.) and how to communicate with the birth parents. Figure out how much information you want to divulge, especially the first couple of contacts. Do this before you go live and definitely before your first contact.

During our adoption journey, we encountered many women, and a couple of men, with unique stories and reasons for considering adoption. While these women were all pregnant, which was their commonality, that is where it ended. Every story and situation was unique and very personal. During our journey and post-adoption, when we shared our adoption story with people, there was a common stereotype of the birth mothers. Most people assumed that the birth mothers were young and addicted to drugs and/or alcohol and didn't have the means to support these children. We also heard very hurtful things such as, "How could any mother give away her child?" These comments and conversations were full of judgment, animus, and disgust. There was a demonizing of and a lack of compassion for these women (and some men) who had to make incredibly difficult decisions. Unfortunately, much of this language and stereotypes are accepted as truths in our culture. These words and feelings also lacked empathy toward our plight to become parents. These people did not understand the gratitude we felt and our unique bond with these birth parents. I can say in no uncertain terms that I have the utmost respect, gratitude, and love for these birth parents. I think of them often, wonder how they are doing, and send them love and well-wishes. In our home, we have the ritual of praying over our meals and we always pray for my children's birth parents. There isn't a day that goes by when I don't thank them for the gift of my children. There isn't a day that goes by when I don't thank God for the gift of being a parent.

Tips on how to handle the long wait to parenthood:

1. Share with each other, family, friends, support groups. Share your impatience. Share your anger. Share your confusion. Share what you're comfortable sharing. It's your story, not theirs.

2. Keep children in your life. Surround yourself and spend time with nieces and nephews, friends' kids, the neighbors' little ones. It's a nice reminder of why you're waiting.

3. Go on vacation. It may well just be your last vacation for a while, so take it. And don't feel guilty. You deserve it. Even if you need to cancel your vacation with the arrival of your child (like our trip to Curacao in the Caribbean, which we still haven't taken yet), you can recoup some of the costs. And it will be worth it in the end.

4. Don't buy any baby stuff. This is so true. I can't even imagine if we started decorating the baby's room as soon as we went live, only to have our hopes dashed one contact after another. That room would have been a daily reminder of our misfortune and our failure in trying to start our family. The exception, of course, is having a car seat available. That should be the only thing you buy.

5. Keep on keeping on. Carry on like normal. If you need to, throw yourself into your work. Find a side business. Volunteer. Pick up a new hobby. The trick is to find whatever it is that will help make the waiting period not feel like waiting. Remember that your child is out there and will come to you when the time is right.

CHAPTER 11

FIRST BIRTH MOTHER CONTACT

O
UR FIRST CONTACT was with Ashleigh from Hollywood, a pregnant mom in her twenties with a four-year-old boy. This call came within the first two months of going live, and from the beginning seemed almost too good to be true. Ashleigh was working and going to school to finish her degree. She was dating the man who was the birth father of her unborn child. He was not the father of her four-year-old but was somewhat involved in raising him. Ashleigh was honest, kind, and up-front. From the beginning, she was transparent about being in contact with other families. She was realistic about her limitations on parenting another child. She was super busy with all her school and work activities. She wanted to stay focused on being a good parent for her son, and felt that trying to raise another child would impede her ability to finish her schooling and get a better job. Ashleigh wanted to make a better life for herself and her son. Her relationship with the birth father was still relatively new, and she wasn't sure where things would go. She was torn up about placing the child for adoption. She loved being a parent, and she *loved* her son. She was about three to four months pregnant and wanted to decide on an adoptive family

so they could start to get to know each other and establish the fundamentals of a long-term relationship. We had many phone conversations with her over several weeks. Our interactions with her were very ordinary.

We were very excited about this prospect. Ashleigh communicated well. She was having a healthy pregnancy and she seemed to be making the decisions for all the right reasons. We were both very excited, yet we were cautious. It seemed to happen easily, and the situation seemed ideal. We interacted with Ashleigh over the phone for several weeks. Then we started to talk about a visit where we would meet her and maybe her son. We got more excited and were looking forward to going to L.A. to meet her in person. We were nervous and anxious to become parents, and yet it seemed so fast. Our interactions with her became less frequent and then, finally, we didn't hear from her again. Ashleigh informed IAC that she had decided on two women from L.A. whom she had recently met.

After this prospect fizzled out, in some way, we were relieved. It's one thing to decide to become parents, and it's entirely something else to start thinking about actually being parents. We didn't feel too disappointed. We figured that it would happen when it was meant to be.

Shortly after our first interaction, I was on a business trip in Atlanta when Lorevic called to inform me that he had a call from a woman wanting to make a decision quickly. He had a great first conversation with her and he was excited about everything he heard. She indicated that she was due in one month and needed to place the baby girl as soon as possible. She stated that there were potentially four different birth fathers, but they were unknown and not involved. After this call, we were both eager to learn more. Potential parents in four weeks—how exciting! The birth mom seemed all in, enthusiastic about our profile and what we could offer as parents. By the time I returned from my trip, she had been in contact with our agency and changed her mind. It was a short, engaging, exciting interaction that was over. We hadn't invested much time and didn't know much about her, so, fortunately, the loss wasn't hard to take.

About a month after this call, a high school junior named Sarah contacted us. Sarah was a Mormon living with her parents and nine siblings in Arizona. She was having a forbidden relationship with a Latino boy in her high school and she was concealing her pregnancy from her family. Sarah was afraid of telling her family about her pregnancy and she wanted to make her own decision without interference from her parents. She was worried that her family would want to keep the child and raise it on their own. We had many interactions with her over a few weeks. They were short and sweet. Mostly texts and IM and some phone interactions, but she showed great interest in us nonetheless. She sent photos of herself and her boyfriend. Thank God for Lorevic, since he is into contemporary music, fashion, and youthful trends. I am more into business and politics. In the case of this Arizona birth mother, he was able to keep the conversation going and find points of common interest during some awkward conversations. She eventually stopped texting and we continued to reach out to find out how she was doing, but never heard back.

Another disappointment. I cried a little bit and kept ruminating about what we did wrong, or if maybe we weren't fit to be parents. God knows there were enough messages from society telling us that two men can't be parents. We already had our self-doubt and then to have birth mothers choose other people made us feel worse. Lorevic is an optimist and was able to shoulder the pain of the disappointment better than me.

We were four months into being "live" in the system. We had already had four contacts with birth mothers and we were starting to feel fatigued. Was this meant to be?

CHAPTER 12

BEING SCAMMED

I T WAS MY birthday weekend, and we decided to go to L.A. to visit some family and celebrate. We were excited for the change of pace and the opportunity to stop thinking about meeting birth parents. We drove down to L.A. on a Friday and arrived late. We went to sleep and woke up to our phones vibrating against the nightstand on Saturday morning before 9 a.m. Mikkaylah was a birth mother and was super interested in us. She had seen our profile on the IAC website and loved our story and photos. We had an initial phone call with her that lasted almost one hour. We talked about everything. Unlike our last experience, which took place primarily over text and IM, this birth mother wanted to talk. I loved this connection because I am more of a talker than a writer. In our first conversation with her, we covered lots of ground. She gave us lots of background on her pregnancy and situation. She also asked us a lot of questions about how we planned to parent and the values we held dear to us. She sounded interested in us as a family, and we were incredibly excited.

After showering and getting ready, we left our hotel room on cloud nine. We met my family for lunch and were oozing with excitement. Later in the day, we received another text from Mikkaylah saying she wanted to chat again. We immediately responded to her text message and got on the phone with her thinking it would last for a few minutes. Our call with Mikkaylah lasted another hour, and she was asking questions about how we would handle certain parenting situations and discipline our child. She also wanted to know our religious beliefs and how we planned to raise the child. There was a certain intensity about the calls that felt different than the calls with other women. Mikkaylah seemed to be quizzing us in a way and digging deep into our personalities. These questions seemed more in line with how the various social workers interacted with us. During that call, she said, "I want you to be my child's parents." We were hesitant and kept telling her that on Monday, we could connect with our social worker at the agency and move things forward. After this call, she sent a text of ultrasound with images of the baby.

We went to sleep that evening tired, scared, exhausted, and over-the-moon excited. It was starting to feel real. The interactions with Mikkaylah were super intense, but they felt very hopeful. On Sunday morning, she called again and we spoke at length. We had already said so much in the previous calls that we were a little unsure why she called back. Nonetheless, we continued to fall in love with the idea that our child was coming to us from this birth mother. We had brunch and got in the car for our long journey home—excited and hopeful about our baby. It had turned out to be such an incredible birthday weekend.

While we were driving home, Mikkaylah called again. We put her on speakerphone as one of us drove, and we both talked. At this point, it didn't feel like there was anything left to say. We had talked with her for almost four hours about everything, education, religion, parenting styles, our families, our personalities, our work, etc. Lorevic was getting exhausted with the interactions. We told Mikkaylah we needed to stop for gas and needed to get off the phone. After we hung up, we looked at each other and asked, "How are we going to continue this intense communication for another four months before the baby arrives?" He is very pragmatic and realistic and said maybe she isn't the one for us.

We were looking for open adoption and wanted to have interactions with the birth families, but we were not looking for a co-parenting situation. We started to talk about how we could manage the next four months with Mikkaylah until the baby was born and then how we would handle interactions with her after birth. Perhaps, Mikkaylah was just excited and nervous and would back off over time. We couldn't wait for Monday morning to talk to our social worker and to get her insights into the situation.

On Monday morning, I arrived in the office and sat in my cube. All of a sudden, a long text message popped up from Mikkaylah. In her message, there was an image of a cross and crazy talk about God and salvation. It contained language about the evils of abortion and homosexuality. I gasped, what the hell was going on? I immediately called Lorevic and told him about the text. He was relieved. He said we couldn't have managed that intensity. Then, we called Annie at IAC and she asked for the phone number. She informed me that this woman was a fraud and that she was not pregnant. It turned out that she was scamming us for attention—what they call an emotional scam. She lived in Pennsylvania and does this frequently. Since she never asks for money, she isn't breaking any laws. The agency warned us that this could happen, but it was incredibly rare. We later learned that people do this with adoptions and missing people. These deranged people know you are vulnerable and desperate for something that they might have, so they draw you into an interaction where they become the center and the keys to your dreams. Mikkaylah had sucked the innocence of our hopes and dreams out of us and made this adoption process a nightmare. This interaction was devastating, and we felt violated. We didn't quite know what to do next.

CHAPTER 13

QUESTIONING OURSELVES

W E FELT VIOLATED and used. We felt terrible and yet determined to meet our child. We were both heartbroken and exhausted. We felt so out of control. We took this set-back very hard. After the last four interactions, we started to wonder if our decision to pursue adoption over surrogacy was the best, and we began to question ourselves.

After processing the situations over a few days, we started to go internal and ask ourselves a lot of questions:

- What were we doing that was not connecting with any of these women?

- Why were we so gullible and good targets for a scam?

- For the first three women, what could we have done to keep them interested?

- Did we not reach out enough?

- Were they looking for something from us? Something that we weren't hearing?
- What did the other couples do that we did not?

With our first, prolonged connection with Ashleigh, we kept our hopes and our excitement from overflowing. We also didn't want to come across as stalkers. We set expectations from the beginning that we would keep communications to a weekly basis and then increase as time went on and we had a chance to meet in person. Maybe we should have been in touch more often? Perhaps it was okay to be stalkers?

This whole process of establishing a relationship with a birth mother was befuddling. Our social worker, Annie, recommended that in general, a minimum of once a week contact is a good plan for a potential birth mom in her first trimester or even second trimester. She suggested that initiating contact twice a week was appropriate, but probably not any more than that. She also recommended that we follow the cues of the birth mother more closely. If she contacted us more often, then that's great! She suggested that we could adjust based on her responses. If she is getting back to you right away and seems excited to talk, then you might be okay to "up" your communication a little bit. If you find yourselves leaving messages and waiting for a day or two for a callback, it is probably a sign that she does not want to talk too often.

In the end, Annie recommended that if we were ourselves in terms of communication, we would find a birth mom who lined up with our values. In a lot of ways, it's similar to dating—some people wait three days after a great date to call, while others text the same night saying, they had a good time! She suggested trying to stick to what feels natural and comfortable to us while letting a potential birth mom know that you are excited to talk and hope to speak again soon. A lot of times, it helps at the end of a conversation to make a plan for when you will connect again. Sometimes, in longer matches, Annie even encouraged people to set up a specific time, like just planning on talking every Sunday at 7 or something similar.

After this flurry of activity in the first four months, things got very quiet for a long time. We had infrequent contacts over the next year. We received two messages from a graduate student who had missed her first period and was maybe six weeks pregnant. She seemed to be more interested in gathering information about adoption and thinking about talking with her boyfriend about the situation. We had another brief interaction with a 49-year-old grandmother from Florida with five children, two older children from her first marriage, and three younger children from her second marriage. She was estranged from her second husband. She was having an affair with the 22-year-old gardener from down the street and found out she was pregnant. She was utterly overwhelmed and had no idea how she was going to manage another child. We talked with her a couple of times and she seemed sincere and credible. We had questions and concerns about her pregnancy due to her age, and we were open to exploring. Then, communication went silent.

In October 2010, my father had a stroke and had some ongoing complications. His stroke and recovery distracted me from the wait for our child in the fall of 2010. During his recovery, I traveled to the Chicago frequently for work and I spent a lot of time with my parents. I was helping my mom take care of Dad and I was spending time with him during his recovery. When we thought Dad was on the road to a full recovery, he was diagnosed with a treatable type of cancer. It was during his illness that I told him how much he meant to me and how I felt about our relationship. He taught me so much about being a good human being and man. He taught me about commitment, responsibility, faith, honesty, hard work, family, and the meaning of sacrifice. I wanted him to meet our child. He loved being a grandfather and he loved Lorevic. I was excited for him to be part of this vital piece of my life. In February 2011, I received a call from my mother that Dad fainted and he was going into the cath lab to have a stent put into his heart. He never emerged from the cath lab, and I was devastated. I felt so much grief. His death shook me greatly. He had always been a balancing force in my life. With his death, I felt lost. His death and the wait for our child was wearing me down.

After my dad's death in February 2011, Lorevic and I decided we wanted to get "married." While the federal or state governments did not recognize same-sex marriage, we wanted our friend who is an Episcopal priest to bless our union. Planning a wedding was a great distraction from my mourning and waiting for our baby. Our friends and extended family members came from around the country to celebrate our commitment and love. Despite the sadness of my dad's passing, it was a joyous occasion. After we said our vows and exchanged rings, we held each other tightly and cried tears of joy for our union.

Two weeks after my dad's death, we had a meaningful contact with an African-American single mother of two girls from Montgomery, Alabama, named Demetria. She was 37 weeks pregnant and expecting in three weeks. We had multiple phone conversations with her and we were very excited. We connected well with her over the phone. Demetria was going to college and barely getting by with her current situation. We were super excited. We were working closely with one of the IAC intake social workers, Katie, in hopes that we would go to Alabama to meet Demetria. As part of the process of working with the adoption agency, they require proof of pregnancy for their services. Katie recommended that we see the proof of pregnancy before we booked our flights. Katie reached out to Demetria several times, and we never heard anything again. While I was still fully grieving Dad's death, this failed contact with a prospective birth mother pushed me into a deeper hole of sorrow.

Over the next 12 months, we had only one contact. In November 2011, we had a brief interaction with Lacie from Knoxville, Tennessee, that fizzled out quickly. During this year, lots of our paperwork and documents expired and we were required to renew our credentials. During this time, we were briefly put on hold because our Livescans had lapsed. Livescans are the electronic fingerprints that are used to check your criminal record across the country. They needed to be redone every year to check for any changes in your criminal status. These are important and necessary for the safety of the children, but it was frustrating and demoralizing to continue to do all this work without any results.

In March 2012, we had another interaction with birth parents that came through our agency. The circumstances of these birth parents were unsettling and unique to all of our other interactions. It was one of the only communications that we had over Skype. They wanted to connect with both audio and visual. All of our other interactions had been phone, text, or email. Many of them sent us photos, but we never did a video chat with anyone else. We scheduled a time to meet with them and then Skyped for about 45 minutes.

The birth mother, Angel, was about four months pregnant and the birth father, Tracy, were in a committed relationship. Both Angel and Tracy were on disability and were looking for financial support during the pregnancy for the next five months. We learned from our agency that it is common to help with expenses in cases where the birth mother can't work due to difficulties with the pregnancy. Our social worker told us this arrangement usually took place in the last trimester of pregnancy. For Angel and Tracy, they were very explicit about the support they wanted, including rent, food, health care, etc. On the one hand, we liked their honesty and transparency. On the other hand, the money seemed paramount to a decision on adoptive parents. Angel and Tracy had a total of eight children, Angel had four children from her previous relationships and Tracy had four children from his previous relationships. They weren't parenting any of these children. This pregnancy was their first child together, and they had no intention of parenting the child. On some level, it felt like they were using the children as tools to generate income for themselves. In all of our previous interactions, we met women who were struggling financially but none who were so concerned about financial support. All the previous women were more concerned with the well-being of the child. With Angel and Tracy, it felt like the well-being of the child was secondary, and their own welfare was of greater importance. We were conscious that our decision to become parents to their birth child was dependent on our willingness to support them financially. This arrangement didn't sit well with us. We wanted our connection to the birth parents to be about their child and not about helping them financially. We decided that this couple was not right for us.

We were starting to grow weary. We re-engaged in our professional lives with greater tenacity and began to connect with friends more frequently. We prayed to God for our child as we tried to keep faith amid the waiting.

With each new contact, our hopes and dreams re-emerged brighter and fuller. We were desperate to become parents and take control of this situation. The waiting and the ups and downs of this journey prepared us for the actual work of parenting. When people embark on parenting, they sometimes think that their children will accept their will and that they can control their kids. But honestly, these beautiful, individual souls come into our world, and we are responsible for them. We love them, and yet we are, in many ways, only guides for their inner being. What I am saying is that, in all honesty, we control very little in the lives of our little ones. Thank goodness they have free will. Our journey to create our family and the lack of control we felt all along the way for our adoption were great parenting and life lessons.

Two years after going live in the system, we were becoming incredibly hopeless. We started to question whether or not becoming parents was in our cards. We began to wonder whether or not God had a plan for us to have a child. We started to ask serious questions about why finding our child was so elusive.

- Why are we not connecting with anyone?
- Why wasn't anyone calling us anymore?

- Why was the dream so fleeting?
- Could we go on in our lives without a child and be happy?
- Was it time to give up hope and move on?

We continued to ask ourselves all of these questions and we continued to hope. Finally, we started to reconsider our decision for adoption. We felt so powerless and we felt out of control. We were unable to make things happen and we decided we wanted to take more action in creating our family. We were desperate. So, we reached out to two friends who were both doctors. Larry is an obstetrician and has experience with delivering children through surrogacy and Jonathon, his husband, is an internist. We scheduled lunch to talk about the surrogacy process and what it was like for the surrogates and the parents. Larry and Jonathon were also considering a family, and were considering surrogacy. This tie to genetics was not essential to us, and we had long decided that it was more important for us that we give back. Our faith in God taught us that there was a child out there who was coming into our family. But after so much time and so much waiting, maybe our thinking was faulty. Perhaps we needed to take control. We could provide the sperm, we could get an egg, and we could make this happen. After this lunch with our friends, we started to reconsider seriously pursuing surrogacy.

CHAPTER 14

EASTER WEEK GIFT

E ASTER SUNDAY WAS quickly approaching. We made plans with Lorevic's family to celebrate Easter and we had brunch. We expressed our sorrow about not being able to find our child and we expressed our dismay about what we were doing. I remember this Easter brunch like it was yesterday. I felt sad and hopeless. I thought that the dream of being parents was out of our reach. I had lost hope that we would find our child and become parents. And then we had our big break.

On the day after Easter in 2012, we received a phone call from IAC and our placement social worker, Karen, told us that there was a family in L.A. that was considering adoption and wanted to talk to us. We were ecstatic and excited about the possibility of finding our child and scared that this would turn out to be another false promise. Karen gave us the birth father's phone number. I remember going into a closed office at work, shutting the door, and thinking to myself, "I hope and I pray that this will work out for us." In the back of my mind, I kept saying to myself, "I can't go on much longer—trying to keep hope alive and not ending up with a child." I picked up the phone and I dialed the number. The phone rang for a bit. My stomach was tied in knots, my hands were clammy, and my heart was beating fast. On the other end of the line, someone picked up, and it was a man. We said hello and we started the conversation. I was surprised to be talking to a man. Justin had a warm and friendly voice. I could tell he was nervous and so was I.

Over the last two years, with every new situation we had always started with birth mothers and we never started our interactions with the birth father. Justin and I had a brief friendly conversation. We talked about why they considered adoption, the birth mom's pregnancy, and their current family situations. I felt cautiously optimistic and relieved that the call was behind me. I immediately called Lorevic and shared every detail. That evening we talked some more and we were more excited. The next day, Justin and I spoke again. We had another great conversation and, this time, it felt more natural and trusting. This situation was so different than every other interaction we had in the past. I felt a greater sense of connection and familiarity. Lorevic had a conversation with Justin, and we both felt good about our interactions. After three days of having multiple phone conversations with Justin, we never talked with the birth mother, and this made us uneasy. Finally, Karen suggested that we go to Los Angeles and meet with the birth parents.

We were freaking out and hopeful and fearful at the same time. During this week, we leaned on each other often. We had been through this process so many times, and we no longer knew what was real. We couldn't believe that we were finally about to meet the birth parents. It had been such a long road and we grew so cynical. What was happening? Was there a real connection between us? Would they meet us? Would we feel nothing? Would they feel nothing? Would the reality of an open adoption be too much for us to handle? Or too much for them to handle? All of these questions were swirling around in our heads and our hearts.

We drove to L.A. on Thursday after work. We arrived at 2 a.m., and, on Friday morning at noon, we met with the birth parents for the first time. We had never spoken with the birth mom over the phone and quite frankly weren't sure what to expect. A social worker from the L.A. office of IAC came to the meeting for introductions and to facilitate the conversation. Over the first two hours, the social worker helped with high-level questions to get us all comfortable with each other and break the ice.

The birth mom's name was Lyla. Since Lyla did not have prenatal care, she was unsure of her exact due date, but she thought she was about eight months pregnant and she knew she was having a girl. Lyla and Justin had been in a committed relationship for the last five years and had one other child together who was about three years old. Lyla also had two other children from an earlier marriage. The L.A.-based social worker needed to leave to handle other responsibilities. We were alone with Justin and Lyla and, over the next three hours, our conversation went more in-depth. We talked about everything under the sun including each of our histories as individuals and then as couples. We felt such a strong connection with them. At the end of almost five hours together, Justin and Lyla turned to us and asked if we would like to adopt their daughter and we immediately said yes. In open adoption lingo, this means we matched with each other. Both birth parents and adoptive parents decided they liked each other and wanted to create an open relationship for the future. We had a magical five hours with them and we felt completely connected. After matching, the birth parents asked us if we'd like to come with them to see an ultrasound the next day and see their child. We were beyond excited. Everything was becoming very real.

Afterward, Lorevic and I went to dinner and talked about every aspect of our conversations. We replayed every detail and everything felt light. We were giddy. We ordered a couple glasses of red wine and had a lovely meal celebrating our match with Justin and Lyla. We went back to our hotel and tried to rest, but we slept very little. We were too excited. We tossed and turned, thinking about the little girl in Lyla's belly who we would see tomorrow.

The next day, we met Lyla, Justin, and their son. We saw the ultrasound and, for the first time, we saw our daughter inside her birth mother's stomach. We were so happy, exhilarated, and couldn't wait to meet her. In the ultrasound, she was curled up and it looked like she was sucking her thumb. While we felt 100% certain that this was our birth family, we were also scared that it would not work out.

Later that evening, we met Lyla and Justin for dinner at Bucca Di Peppo in Redondo Beach. We continued to build a trusting, loving, and fulfilling relationship with them. It was such a great evening. The stress of the match and the ultrasound were behind us. We were able to relax and connect with them on a deeper level. We were no longer talking to each other with the nervousness of a making a decision about matching. We were entering into a new phase of the relationship. In some ways, it felt like we were all the parents or extended family talking about the baby's future in such a caring, loving manner. It no longer felt like we were strangers, and our relationship became very intimate. As I wrote this paragraph seven years after that dinner, tears streamed down my face as I thought about this special relationship. It is a relationship unlike any other relationship in my life. We have so much gratitude and love for Lyla and Justin. Despite all the uncertainty, we fell in love with them and were so ready for the next steps.

But looking back at our long journey and each birth mother holistically, each one was on their own odyssey to get to their big decision. It all started with a realization of where they were at in their lives and whether or not they could give their child the experience that they wanted and deserved. They were steeling themselves to make the ultimate sacrifice, making the hardest decision they would ever make in their lives. From the young woman who was in college but missed her period to the 49-year-old grandmother with five children, these women and men were willing to give us the greatest gift in the world. Freely and wholeheartedly. It's a constant reminder that birth moms and birth dads are to be cherished and to remind our children where they came from and why they are so special.

And maybe all this waiting is by design. Maybe there's a lesson to be learned or relearned, not just for us but for our children. Maybe good things come to those who wait? I wholeheartedly believe what they say about adoptions—that you get the child that you were always meant to get. I know it's true for us. At the time, our daughter was the best thing that ever happened to us, and today, we can also include our son as one of the best things to happen to our family.

PART 4

FOREVER FAMILY

CHAPTER 15

OUR DAUGHTER IS BORN

AFTER OUR LONG journey to match with Lyla and Justin, we were ready to begin the next phase of the process, which meant getting ready for an infant and becoming parents. We hadn't done anything to prepare for our new lives as parents because we didn't know when it would happen. We didn't get the baby room ready or buy any baby stuff. On top of the lack of necessary baby paraphernalia, we were advised not to get prepared for the baby because it would make the wait seem much longer. With that said, we had nothing and we hadn't read any parenting books either. It had seemed premature. But now that the time was imminent, we needed to figure out how to be parents. We both grew up in large families and were around lots of kids. Lorevic had a lot more experience with children because he lived close to his family and was around when his sisters started having children. For me, I was always visiting Chicago and spending time with my nieces and nephews, yet I rarely baby-sat them. In my mind, I was a great uncle when it came to remembering birthdays and special occasions and giving lots of love, but didn't have a lot of experience with changing dirty diapers, middle-of-the-night feedings, or soothing whining kids. The idea of being responsible for an infant was a little scary. Instinctively, I felt well suited for an infant but didn't know how I would perform when it happened.

On Sunday afternoon, we began the long drive home. We were on cloud nine and beyond excited. After spending time with Lyla and Justin, they indicated that the baby was likely due in about three weeks. We returned home feeling like we had some time to ready ourselves for this next phase of the process.

We returned home late that Sunday afternoon. I took the following day off from work to think about everything we needed to do to prepare for parenthood. On Monday, early in the afternoon, we received a call from Justin that Lyla's blood pressure was high and she was being admitted to the hospital to give birth. WHAT? We both thought we had a few weeks to prepare. This news was the beginning of our world of uncontrollable factors with our children. We had nothing in our house to take care of a child. I hadn't made it to Babies R Us yet. The only thing that we had for an infant was a car seat, which was required as part of the home study and adoption approval process. We could drive our baby home from the hospital, but once at home, there was nothing to take care of her. It was almost surreal. I drove to the Babies R Us and bought a bassinet to use next to the bed. I also purchased formula, bottles, and diapers. I returned home and quickly put together the bassinet. Lorevic was still at work when all of this was happening. He came home after 5 and we went to have dinner before we began the drive back to L.A. It was our last real meal as a parentless couple. We ordered dinner and chatted and connected. We had no idea what we were in for over the next few days or years. After dinner, we jumped in the car and started driving to L.A. It had only been 24 hours since we got home.

Over the next six hours, we talked about our expectations for the next few days and we talked about the short-term needs for childcare. One of the hardest things about adoption is the lack of the ability to plan. When you get the call, you either say yes and adjust to the situation or you say no and miss out on the opportunity to be parents. We had talked generally about taking time off for bonding, but those conversations were all very vague because we didn't know when it was going to happen. As we were driving down to L.A., we both talked about our current workloads and who would take leave first and second. We felt lucky to live in California, which has state laws that provide for protected paternity leave and to work for companies that provided time for adoption leave. I was ramping down on several projects and almost done. Lorevic, on the other hand, was in the thick of some significant deliverables and couldn't stop working. I called my boss and told him about the situation. He was supportive and excited as I had been sharing our journey along the way.

During the six-hour drive, we spent a lot of time talking about her name. We hadn't thought about it very much because we didn't know if we would be able to name our daughter. Birth parents often want to name their children before adoption placement. We hadn't talked with Lyla and Justin yet about it, but we needed to come up with some names. During this conversation, we spoke about the decision for the surname for our kids. I didn't feel tied to my last name. It isn't the prettiest name—it's long and a little clunky. I have two brothers and several nephews who would carry on the family name. My father had passed away already, and he had expressed that he wouldn't care about his surname being carried on for our child. When my father was living, I talked to him a couple of times about changing my last name, and he was supportive. Lorevic was the only son in his family and, if we decided to use his surname, our children would be the only children with the family name. I loved and respected his parents so much and I thought that giving our daughter their family name would mean a lot to them. I loved my husband's last name, and I often thought about taking his name after we were married. In the end, we used Lorevic's last name for our daughter, which meant I got to pick her first name.

I wanted to pick a first name that had two syllables, so her name could be adapted over time for the different phases of our daughter's life and allow her to express her personality through her name. I wanted a name that connected my child with my Irish heritage, which I always identified with strongly. I started my search in Irish girl names and came up with a long list of options. I quickly narrowed down on Caitlin. When I searched the meaning of Caitlin, I came across Saint Caitlin, who was considered a mythical person of great powers who helped the Irish people throw off the tyranny of the British empire. She was a sort of like Joan of Arc—sturdy, strong, and unafraid. This name resonated with how I wanted my daughter to grow up in the world. Based on Lyla's heritage being related to the Hawaiian culture, we wanted her name to be spelled with a K instead of a C because K is very prominent in the Hawaiian language. We still didn't know how Lyla and Justin felt about the naming, but we were prepared if they wanted us to pick her name.

During our journey to Southern California, we spoke with family and friends to share the news. We didn't call too many people as we had trepidations about what would happen over the coming days and weeks. We had stopped talking about the process to so many people because we had become so weary. We were heading to L.A. on our own—no other family, just us. This trip alone symbolized how we had done so many things in our lives, together as a couple. Often when someone is having a baby, lots of families come to the hospital to be there for the parents. For us, neither of our families had experienced adoption and weren't familiar with how things would happen. We were very unsure of what to expect and didn't want to worry about other family member's expectations. We had developed this life together on our own, and we didn't ask for help from others. What we didn't know at the time was that this would change with parenting. Bottom line: parenting a newborn requires help from others. We hadn't experienced many situations in our lives that we needed help outside ourselves and we were self-sufficient. Our parents and families were excited for us, but we could also sense trepidation in their enthusiasm. Adoption was a foreign concept to them and they didn't know how it would fit into their lives.

We didn't know how quickly things were unfolding and went straight to Little Company of Mary Hospital in Torrance at 2 a.m. We didn't know where we would sleep that night and prepared ourselves for the beginning of sleepless nights. We were concerned about how things would play out at the hospital due to the discrimination faced by LGBTQ people by the Catholic Church. We didn't know if this hospital followed the doctrine of the Church and we had no idea how they would handle an adoption by a same-sex couple. We anticipated that there might be some reluctance. At the time, we were practicing Catholics and were well aware of the Church's teaching condemning homosexuality. I didn't know how the Church was putting their homophobia into policy and practice in California and its hospitals.

When we entered Little Company of Mary Hospital and arrived on the birthing floor, we were welcomed with open arms by the hospital staff. They gave us a room right next door to the birth mom, so we would be available immediately if our baby arrived. Our fears about discriminatory treatment didn't happen and the hospital staff exceeded all our expectations. It was a lesson in how sometimes we anticipate being treated differently due to past experiences, and how these fears can be overblown.

We felt touched to be right next door to Lyla and Justin. On the one hand, it felt strange to be next door to Lyla, we had just met four days ago—it felt too fast, too soon, and like we hadn't earned the trust yet to be included. On the other hand, it felt like we were becoming an extended family. After settling into the hospital room, we were both too excited to sleep very much. On top of that, the sofa couch was uncomfortable. Either way, it didn't matter to us. We were one step closer to meeting our daughter and we couldn't feel any happier.

Later that morning, after only a little sleep, we woke with great excitement but also fear and anxiety. We were educated about the birth parents' rights and their ability to change their minds along the way. While we felt confident about our connection with them, we just had no experience and no understanding of what it must have felt like for them. We were aware of two situations where children were placed with adoptive families and then reclaimed by their birth families. One case was a gay couple from

San Francisco named Brian and Fernando, who were our friends. Brian and Fernando had matched with a birth mother in Michigan and traveled there for the birth. They had taken the baby with them to their hotel while they waited for the mandated two-week waiting period to leave the state. They fell in love and were getting ready to leave when the birth mother was persuaded by her parents to take the child back, so the grandparents would raise the child. Brian and Fernando were devastated by this experience and had felt so much pain and grief. While these situations were rare, they did happen, and it was a real risk for us.

We spent the morning eating breakfast and trying to remain calm. We had no idea how things would play out over the coming days. We were waiting for Lyla to wake up and let us know how she wanted us to take part in her delivery. We were shopping at the gift shop and buying our first onesie for our daughter. We didn't want to go far away. We spent time in the chapel praying for the unknown, the delivery of our daughter, and the safety of Lyla. We prayed for the feelings of heartbreak and sadness that we anticipated the birth parents would feel. We prayed thanksgiving for the gift of our daughter and we prayed that our hearts wouldn't break. All of these prayers continued over the next several months and years.

In the afternoon, we talked about naming our daughter. Our agency had given us lots of paperwork to help us through the process and they had been in contact with Lyla and Justin to inform them of the steps as they, too, were learning this for the first time. When a baby is born, the infant takes on the last name of the birth parent. Some birth parents want to name the baby as a way to connect and bond with him or her. We had decided on a name and were open to figuring it out with Lyla and Justin. They told us that we should name her since we would be her parents. We told them about how we chose the name Kaitlyn and they loved the story. This gesture was one of many signs of their commitment to us being her parents. There were many other signs throughout the next couple of days that demonstrated their commitment to us and their respect for our parenting decisions.

Throughout that afternoon, I was on the phone with my family sharing my excitement and my fear. My mom and sister were worried about me and asked my brother, Bill, who lives in the greater L.A. area to check in on me. It was a pleasant surprise, and he was able to meet Lyla and Justin. It felt terrific to have this community of people behind us, supporting us as we navigated through the uncertainty. Lyla was doing well as she prepared to give birth. She was comfortable with minimal pain. She was excited, nervous, and very engaged. We learned more about her life and the entire family during these hours that we waited for the delivery of our daughter. Her last birthing experience was challenging and she experienced great pain. Justin warned us that Lyla could become irritable and we should be prepared to see a different side of her as the pain increased. Regardless, Lorevic and I felt so blessed to be part of her delivery. We were able to understand better what women and mothers go through to bring life into the world.

When the doctor hurried into the room for the delivery, Lyla had Lorevic move to the foot of the bed as she started to push. Kaitlyn came into the world and the doctor handed her to Lorevic to hold. With hands trembling from joy, I cut the umbilical cord. Lorevic handed Kaitlyn to me and I held my daughter for the first time. I fell in love with her in an instant. It was amazing.

It was terrific that we were able to embrace her first. Lyla and Justin had made their decision and wanted us to experience all the first events as if we had given birth to her ourselves. It was one of the greatest joys I had ever felt in my life. We cried with happiness and held her tightly.

Kaitlyn was weighed, measured, and tested for all functions. Everything checked out perfectly. After the doctor finished his exam, he handed Kaitlyn to Lyla and we watched her embrace her. She looked at Kaitlyn with such love and devotion. Lyla talked about her other children and how they looked and behaved in the hours after birth. Lyla could see herself and Justin in Kaitlyn. Lyla expressed so much joy and happiness, yet I could only imagine how she was feeling inside.

During this time, the nurses came into the room and told us to feed Kaitlyn. We hadn't thought about the details of taking care of her in the first minutes and hours after her birth. Frankly, we didn't know how frequently she would need to be fed. I remember Lyla asking us if we wanted her to breastfeed her. I felt this tingle of fear come into my stomach. We had responded no that we wanted to feed Kaitlyn and take care of her. At that moment, I felt a sense of regret and disappointment from Lyla as if we were taking away something that she wanted to do to bond with Kaitlyn. But it felt too intimate for me, and I selfishly wanted to take on that role.

By this time, it was close to midnight. Lyla was exhausted and ready to sleep. Again, we didn't know what to do. Our social worker told us that it is common for birth mothers and fathers to want to have the first day and night with the child before placement. We were open to whatever Lyla and Justin felt was necessary. We wanted to honor and respect all of their wishes to help them through the transition of carrying this child for nine months to placing her with us. As we prepared to leave the room, Lyla said she wanted Kaitlyn to spend her first night outside her womb with us. We were overjoyed. We knew this child would be the center of our world for the rest of our lives. It became evident and scary that we would have the responsibility of parenting her forever. It had been so theoretical until this moment and then the weight of the responsibility hit me.

We took Kaitlyn next door and began the process of learning how to take care of an infant. Thank God for the nurses. They showed us how to hold, feed, change, and soothe her. It was a quick lesson and then they left the room. Lorevic and I stared at her with amazement. She was cute, innocent, vulnerable, and so full of life. This precious child didn't fuss or cry. She exuded a sense of peacefulness and was sweet beyond belief. We held her for a very long time and then put her into the bassinet so we could get some sleep. We were so exhausted and it was just the beginning. But we couldn't sleep that night. We also needed to wake every two to three hours to feed her and change her. We each took shifts to attend to our daughter and then the other would try to sleep. We wanted to make sure that we met all of her needs.

It all felt really miraculous. Becoming a parent was never supposed to happen to me. When I first came out as gay, I cried for the loss of the possibility of becoming a parent. As I was holding Kaitlyn and looking back on everything that I had overcome to get to this place, it not only felt glorious to be holding this beautiful child in my arms, but it also felt gratifying to conquer my internal obstacles to pursue this dream and overcome so much from the outside world. It was a moment in time that I will forever remember and cherish: Lorevic and I, standing side by side as partners in the beautiful journey to become parents. I am pretty sure we acted like any other first-time parents who were worried about making a mistake. For two men, we felt a very high level of urgency to prove that we could be good parents. Gay dads often feel like they need to overcompensate for the fact that they are not mothers, and we certainly felt inadequate.

In the morning, the nurses came in and showed us how to bond with our daughter through skin-to-skin contact. We took our shirts off and took off her onesie and laid her on our skin. Kaitlyn nuzzled her face into our chests and she felt our heartbeats. We spent the morning together as a family. This was the first day of many days to come when we shared time as a family. These moments were heavenly. The love, safety, and security were palpable.

After the morning, we brought Kaitlyn over to Lyla. We wanted them to spend time together, bonding and getting to know each other. We wanted to honor and respect the nine months while Kaitlyn was in-utero. It was tough for me to leave her there. While we knew we had a secure connection with the birth parents and they were very decisive on us being parents, we also had this fear hanging over our heads that our daughter could stay with her birth family at any point. We felt so protective of her and so attached. She was so small, innocent, and helpless. We wanted to protect her, and we also wanted to protect ourselves.

After we left Kaitlyn with Lyla, we went out of the hospital for a few hours to eat and take some time for ourselves. We kept coming back to thinking about Kaitlyn and wondering how she was doing. We tried to remain calm and let go of the uncontrollable. It was especially hard for me.

I felt scared and anxious. We had spent the night with this beautiful child and fell in love quickly. I could only imagine how it must have felt for Lyla and Justin to hold her, see themselves in her, fall in love with her, and realize that they would not see her precious face every day. This reality was in my head as we spent the time apart from her. It felt so scary to me.

When we returned to see Kaitlyn, I was so relieved. Lorevic seemed okay with the separation from our daughter. My stomach felt twisted in knots, and it felt like it had been a lifetime. When we walked into the room, Kaitlyn and Lyla were very content together. Lyla relayed the events of the day. Kaitlyn liked to eat and had no problems taking the bottle. She was peaceful and content. She fell asleep easily. These were all the standard concerns of a caretaker, and we felt great that everything had gone so well. Lyla said she felt comfortable with her farewell to Kaitlyn, and she was ready for us to take her back. I can only imagine how hard that moment was for her. She played it off coolly and calmly. If I were in her shoes, I would have been wailing and in total despair.

That evening, the hospital staff brought us a special meal with champagne to celebrate the birth of our daughter. This meal is typically given to the birth parents to celebrate a new life, the completion of a safe delivery, and the beginning of the child's life. The staff delivered that meal to us instead of Lyla and Justin. We felt so honored and we felt so loved by the hospital staff. We also felt some remorse and sadness that the birth parents did not have this meal. Despite this sense of sorrow, we had a fantastic first meal together as a family as we were all adjusting to each other. Everything was falling into place, and we would be taking Kaitlyn home in the morning. Lorevic and I were adjusting to this new dynamic between us. Everything felt so natural and perfect. I laid my head on the pillow that evening with so much love and happiness in my heart. I was also pinching myself because, in some way, I couldn't believe that my dreams were coming true.

CHAPTER 16

PARENTING BEGINS

O N THURSDAY MORNING, we woke up with excitement and fear. We had this significant milestone ahead of us for the day. We needed both parties to sign the temporary placement agreement called the Adoption Placement Agreement. The Adoption Placement Agreement is a six-month contract between the birth parents and the prospective adoptive parents. This document allows the prospective adoptive parents to take custody and leave the hospital with the baby. During the first six months, another more critical action needs to happen, which is the signing of the relinquishment of the baby to the adoption agency, state, or county social services department. In California, birth parents are not allowed to sign relinquishments while in the hospital. This law protects the birth parents from poor decision-making in the days immediately following the birth. We left the hospital with the temporary agreement, and then the adoption agency would follow up with the birth parents to sign the relinquishments. The legal aspects of the adoption were foreign to us and something we didn't understand until we were in the middle of the situation or toward the end.

IAC had provided the documents and walked us through the process. The hospital social worker came to meet with us and have us sign the paperwork. While we logically understood the process, getting the signatures and leaving the hospital with our daughter felt scary. My thoughts kept drifting back to birth parents changing their minds. A few questions kept popping into my head—would they let us take her home? Would they change their mind? What could go wrong? How would I handle the situation if our daughter wasn't able to come home with us? My stomach was tied in knots and my heart was racing. I felt so overwhelmed with so many emotions and fear. Amid all this angst, I felt faith in the birth parents, the process, ourselves as a couple, and God. The right thing would happen to us and we needed to believe. It was often hard to have faith. I looked outside myself and our situation to a higher power to get us through the next six months and, later, with the adoption of our son.

In all this angst and process, the hospital photographer came to take family photos. We had no idea that this was something that happened in hospitals. We were so excited to take these photos that captured the joy of becoming parents so beautifully. None of the worry or concern came through in these photos, and the pure joy is painted all over our faces. We have some of the pictures hanging in our house, and every time that I glance at them, it brings me back to the awe I experienced over those days.

After completing all our paperwork, photos, and goodbyes, we got ready for the long drive home to Oakland with our daughter. As we prepared to leave the hospital and get into the car, we looked at our daughter. She seemed so small and innocent to be entering the world. It felt scary to take her outside the comfort of the hospital, a place where we had experienced so much love and kindness in the last three days. When we were ready to leave, the hospital administrators informed us that California law requires children to be carried out of the hospital in the hands of one of the parents sitting in a wheelchair. The safety of the baby and birth mother are paramount and the reason for this law. It felt extraordinary for us since we hadn't given birth as this tradition is reserved for the birth mother. At that moment, my husband and I looked at each other and said, "Who's gonna do this?" I raised my hand quickly and agreed to play the role of mom, which is a role I admired for so long.

It was foreshadowing to many situations that would happen in the years ahead. In this culture with defined father and mother roles, in many cases, one of us would be stepping into the role of mother for our children. This experience brought to the forefront the differences between same-sex and heterosexual couples. Because there are not explicit roles for two men or two women raising a baby, there is a constant defining of roles. In my opinion, this is one of the best aspects of being same-sex parents. Same-sex parents get to figure it out together, do the things that are important to each parent, and ditch society-defined roles. This action of sitting down in the wheelchair to hold my daughter made me identify with my female side, which felt powerful and uplifting. I had always wanted to be a parent and give birth, which is impossible, but now I had the opportunity to be a mother and a father to my daughter. It was an exciting realization.

We left Torrance in the early afternoon while the traffic was manageable. We drove slowly back to Oakland with one of us sitting next to our daughter while the other drove and switching off periodically to change diapers and feed her. This pattern of switching and sharing would become a pattern that would follow us through the rest of our lives. It is one of the best aspects of being partners in parenting.

We arrived home on a Thursday evening to a beautiful welcome from my best friend, Jeff, who would become an uncle and godfather to our children. While we were away, he worked with other friends to get a plethora of baby stuff we would need to raise an infant. When we came into our house, dinner was ready, and we celebrated the arrival of our daughter with a birthday cake with a candle. It was a fantastic evening to re-enter into reality as parents. We spent the rest of the weekend nesting as a family and getting to know this incredible little girl, Kaitlyn.

I loved that weekend at home together with our daughter. It was intimate and connected the three of us. I got an inkling of insight into our changing relationship. My husband and I started to interact differently with the addition of our daughter into our lives.

At the end of the weekend, my husband returned to work, and I started my paternity leave. My paternity leave was an incredible gift for me, my daughter, my husband, and our family. It was nice to be able to entirely focus on Kaitlyn's needs and growing into my role as a parent. During my paternity leave, I completely disconnected from work and was fully present for my Kaitlyn. My time at home allowed me to make adjustments to our living space to accommodate our daughter. I handled the other mundane tasks associated with adding a new member to the family, such as pediatrician appointments, insurance coverage, etc. For Lorevic, my role as the primary caretaker allowed him the headspace to complete some big projects at work.

Kaitlyn was incredibly easy. She did all the things that babies do—lots of sleeping, eating, needing diaper changes, and being endlessly held. We fell into a routine of taking walks in the mornings in our neighborhood or around Lake Merritt, a beautiful large tidal lagoon in the center of Oakland. Most days, I packed up the car and we headed out of the house for a few hours. We spent the afternoons at home with three-hour naps and a break for me to take care of myself and the house. I loved the nesting time and being home with her. Lorevic came back excited to learn what developments had happened during the day and we spent time as a family. From 10 p.m. to the morning, I set my alarm and woke up every three hours to feed her. The evening feedings exhausted me and I wasn't prepared for the toll they took on me. After about six to eight weeks, our daughter started to sleep for about five to six hours between feedings. That longer sleep helped me feel better. During my leave, I started reading a lot of parenting books and learning more about how to raise a healthy child.

When we first started feeding our daughter, the hospital gave us formula, since we were unable to breastfeed. We hadn't thought about breastfeeding at all since we couldn't do it ourselves. While at home and learning about healthy parenting, I read a lot about the importance of breast milk and started to second-guess some of my parenting choices. It was just one of the ways I fixated on my perceived inadequacies as a parent and not being a mother. At the time, we lived in the Berkeley area, and breastfeeding was the norm for "healthy" children. I started to become obsessed with the idea of providing our daughter with breast milk. I spent a lot of time trying to figure out the pros and cons of giving her breast milk. I did research on the health benefits from breastfeeding and there were many, which included possible reduction of disease risks such as heart disease and diabetes, the potential to make children smarter, and helping children with healthy weight. Lots of women produce excess breast milk and donate it to babies who don't have access to breast milk. I was considering buying breast milk for Kaitlyn, though I learned that it would cost about $200 per week. In the end, I relied on my mother for help in making some of my parenting decisions—including this one. During my mother's time, breastfeeding was not the standard. She informed me that I had been formula fed along with all of my siblings. When I learned this and that many healthy children all over the world were fed formula, I became comfortable with my daughter continuing on formula.

This episode of questioning my parenting was something that I would continue to experience periodically throughout my life as a parent. There is so much conflicting information about the best child-rearing practicing and, at times, it is hard to figure out what is the best thing to do. Other times, it is tough to put those best practices into realities.

Another issue that would be present throughout my years as a parent came to the surface. For men raising children, there is a societal message that you are not the primary caretaker and you need to defer to the mother. There is a dominant culture of the mother being the primary and best parent in our childcare, schools, and overall society. In many cases, the father is viewed as the secondary parent and not as competent with parenting skills. This mother culture is changing slowly, but there is a powerful message that women are the experts in child-rearing. For two men raising a child, we internalized many of these messages and overcompensated as parents. We wanted and tried to do everything better so we could prove to the world that two men are just as competent as a woman raising a child. We experienced some of this messaging from family members, friends, and childcare professionals, which was hurtful. I never blamed these individuals for their behavior because they were, in many cases, wholly unaware. And, in most cases, they were also victims of the societal construct that provided these messages. At times, these messages are very subtle and, at other times, the messages are straightforward. All you need to do is pick up a parenting magazine, and you will find that most messaging is to mothers.

CHAPTER 17

WAITING FOR RELINQUISHMENTS

WHILE ALL OF the adjustments to parenting were happening, we were waiting for the relinquishment documents to be signed. For the first few weeks, Karen, our placement social worker, told us that it is entirely reasonable for the birth parents not to sign the papers. Many birth parents need time to process their feelings associated with the placement of their child into an adoptive family. Karen told us that relinquishments usually happen in three to six weeks after birth. In the first couple of weeks after arriving home, we didn't think much about relinquishments because we were so focused on taking care of Kaitlyn and we felt connected to Lyla and Justin. Then, our communication with them stopped and they didn't respond to calls or texts. We were worried about the change in our relationship with them and their decision.

Karen was making attempts to get Lyla and Justin to sign the documents through phone calls and more formal communications. They were experiencing some of the same challenges that we were experiencing. I became apprehensive about what was happening for the birth parents and what would happen to us. Without the ability to communicate with them directly, my mind started to go into a very dark place. Perhaps it was related to the lack of sleep and the constant demands of taking care of an infant. Every second of every day, I was becoming more attached to my daughter. She had become my entire world. I was terrified that something could happen to her. I was in frequent contact with Karen. She was very supportive and understanding of my concerns. She had many years of experience with these situations, and she talked me off the ledge many times.

Without the relinquishments signed, we were still in a temporary custody situation, which felt tenuous and nerve-wracking. There were days or moments in the day when I looked into Kaitlyn's eyes and anticipated that she might be gone. These moments I relied on my faith in our relationship with Lyla and Justin and God's plan to keep me going. The Adoption Placement Agreement was time-bound for six months, so things would come to a head in a few months. There was also a part of me that wasn't worried about the ambiguity of the situation. I believed that if the birth parents were going to change their minds, that they would have done that in the immediate days after her birth. As each day passed, it felt less probable that our daughter would be reclaimed.

Karen and other staff at the adoption agency continued to try to connect with the birth parents. As time progressed, their requests became more formal and serious. We were hopeful that the situation would be resolved amicably. During this time, Justin signed the relinquishments while we waited for Lyla. As my time of parental leave came to an end, I started to prepare for the adjustment of working and parenting. My husband was unable to take paternity leave immediately, and we had to come up with a plan for our daughter's care for three to four weeks. We were able to patch together care provided by my sister-in-law and my husband's mother. This situation would be the first of many cases where we would rely on others for help. A significant challenge with a temporary placement agreement is the restrictions placed on caretakers. Only people who had been approved by social services were allowed to care for our daughter for an extended time. Overnights with relatives were not allowed. These restrictions made the childcare more difficult during this time. Many new parents rely on grandparents when they return to work and, at times, children spend the evenings or overnights there when parents needed to travel for business. This help was not an option for us. We had long commutes and had lots of disruption during this time.

I was happy to return to work to keep myself busy and focused, which helped me from thinking about our precarious custody situation with our daughter. I was grateful when Lorevic started his paternity leave. First, there was a tremendous sense of relief about the day-to-day care and something happening to Kaitlyn. While she was in good hands with our family, I felt happier when she was with my husband. I was so pleased that he was having the time to bond with her without the distractions of work. When he started his paternity leave in August 2012, our daughter was three and a half months old. She was beginning to come alive and engaged in the world. Over the next three months, while he was home with her, she would hit many milestones such as sitting up, starting solid food, etc. It was a time of tremendous growth and development.

During my husband's paternity leave, we started the process of figuring out childcare for our daughter, which turned out to be a significant endeavor. The Bay Area childcare environment is complicated and expensive. There are many choices from nanny, home day-care, institutional day-care, and family. We thoroughly researched all the options. Then we interviewed caretakers and day-cares. We landed on a lesbian from Southern California who had just moved to the Bay Area to take care of our daughter at our home. We were ready to both go back to work.

During the temporary placement, we took our first family vacation to Hawaii to attend the wedding of some friends who were also adopting a child. Their placement process had gone much smoother and faster. They knew all the ins-and-outs of the system and were a tremendous support and help. Due to the temporary placement agreement, we were not able to leave California without permission and had to complete a travel form. This paperwork was another reminder that things were still up in the air with the adoption and made it difficult to relax fully. It was such a fantastic trip. We spent a lot of time in the water playing with her and spending time as a family.

The temporary agreement was coming to an end in a few weeks. We were anxious to move past this chapter of uncertainty in our life. Karen explained that if a birth parent did not sign the relinquishments, there can be a claim of abandonment, which can be treated as a misdemeanor or a crime. Throughout this entire process, IAC was responsible for handling all interactions with Lyla and Justin related to the legal requirements. It was a challenging situation because we wanted to keep our long-term open relationship with the birth parents while the agency was trying to comply with the adoption laws. The deadline of the six-month agreement passed, and we weren't sure what was going to happen next. On Halloween day, about six and a half months after our daughter was born, we got the news that Lyla had signed the relinquishments. We learned from Karen that Lyla always knew we were the adoptive parents she wanted and she never intended to change her mind but she just couldn't get herself to sign the paperwork. We cried tears of joy and celebrated by taking our daughter trick-or-treating through the neighborhood. This event was one of the most significant milestones of our life as parents.

Things were not complete because we still needed to finalize the adoption, but a huge weight was lifted off our shoulders. The process moving forward was filled with paperwork, lawyers, judges, etc. but we had overcome the most significant hurdles. We felt much better about claiming our rights to our daughter, and our family was not in jeopardy of being pulled apart. There were so many lessons we learned during these six months. We learned to let go and trust the unknown. We learned that we couldn't control things outside of our life and we couldn't push to move items forward.

We learned to love blindly without guarantees. We learned to rely on each other more deeply. We learned a more profound sense of faith in others, the unknown, and God. We became more resilient. As we faced setbacks along the way, we had to push through our fears, find hope amid uncertainty, and continue to move things forward.

CHAPTER 18

TAKING SHAPE AS A FAMILY

O VER THE NEXT six to seven months, we continued to adapt to raising a child and waiting for the adoption finalization. During this period, we began to regain the long view of our lives together and to build our family life. While we were mired in the paperwork details of finalizing the adoption, our minds and hearts were free from worry about the uncertainty of our adoption status. I remember this time with great fondness. We let out a huge sigh of relief and enjoyed our time together as a family. This was a special time of development for our daughter as she started to become so aware and engaged in the world. We celebrated many firsts, including Thanksgiving, Christmas, and our daughter's first birthday. So many celebrations and so much growth as a family on all levels.

It took another six months before we stood in the Los Angeles County courtroom where Angelina Jolie and Brad Pitt finalized their adoptions with the same judge. When we took the oath to finalize our adoption, it was somewhat anticlimactic. By that time, it had been almost four years since we started the process. The long wait made us tired, and it seemed like we had been carrying the responsibility of parenting for much longer than our one-year-old daughter.

For the finalization ceremony, we traveled down to L.A. in our car, which brought back so many memories from our previous trips to L.A. It became a metaphor for our adoption journey and took a spiritual realm for us. The drive is full of twists and turns, ups and downs, stretches of open space, and that sometimes makes it feel like time is moving too slowly. It was great to be on the other side of these trips. During our previous two visits, we were so excited and anxious on so many levels. This trip was very different—calm and serene. It reminded me of tying a bow on a beautiful box—the final step.

For our journey to LA, it was the three of us together with no other family or friends. We had become such a close and bonded family unit. We didn't know what to expect for the adoption finalization, so we played it low key. We invited our families to join us but didn't make a big fuss about them coming. When we arrived at the courthouse, other families were there to finalize their children's adoptions. Most of these families had large groups of people to celebrate with them. On one level, this made me feel sad and like we had missed out on celebrating a key milestone. There was also a feeling of intimacy with the three of us that made me feel delighted. We were building this family unit together and there was a connection and closeness that felt very pure when we were alone together. Throughout parenting, there are so many first-time events and so many opportunities to celebrate. As first-time parents, it isn't easy to know which ones are the most important to observe. For our daughter's adoption finalization at the courthouse in LA, it didn't feel like the critical celebration.

The key celebration was her first birthday and her adoption finalization party, where we invited over 100 friends and family. For this celebration, my mother and aunt came from Chicago to celebrate with my husband's family. All the friends who supported us along the way came as well. My mother's friends were sending cards and gifts, which made us feel so loved. It felt extraordinary to have this extensive network of people all over the country who were showering us with love. It was so unexpected to have all of these people stepping forward to help.

This incredible love and support also made me feel sad. I experienced many personal milestones as a gay man before becoming a parent—key events that were never celebrated like the birth of our daughter. Perhaps I had kept these accomplishments to myself or a small group of family and friends because the broader culture was uncomfortable with the milestones for LGBTQ single people. When I became a parent and started to have similar parenting experiences as my straight family and friends, I realized how much people did not understand me as a gay man. There was never ill intent but rather a lack of awareness on the essential milestones for queer people. On my part, there was a lack of desire to educate them on some of the landmarks. Once we had our daughter, my husband and I were all of a sudden included in a much larger heterosexual community. We now had something much more in common with our heterosexual friends. We also noticed that we had one less thing in common with our gay friends.

Over the coming years, we encountered an identity crisis of sorts. We were now parents and taking care of our daughter became front and center for most of our lives. Outside of work, we focused most of our time around her and family time. This transition is typical for all new parents. The difference for us was that none of our gay friends had kids. We were changing priorities and their preferences remained the same. In the past, a lot of our common bonds with our gay friends involved socializing through going to parties, bars, dinners, and travels. While we still connected with friends on occasion to socialize in the gay scene, the majority of the time we wanted to spend time with our daughter and the family.

One of the starkest reminders of our changing relationships came when our friends, Ethan and Tom, invited us to their July 4th pool party. We were excited to go and catch up with a large group of friends we hadn't seen in several months. On top of seeing old friends, we were excited to go to their house because they lived in the East Bay Hills with a huge backyard and pool overlooking the San Francisco Bay where Kaitlyn could swim and play. At the time, we were living in a townhouse with no backyard. Initially, we accepted the invitation and planned on attending as a family. As the date approached, we emailed Ethan and Tom to let them know that we would be arriving late to accommodate Kaitlyn's nap. That's when they told us that children were not welcome. WOW. We were surprised and disappointed to hear that our daughter was not welcome. We faced a dilemma of finding a babysitter so we could go to Ethan and Tom's party, or spending the holiday with our daughter. It was a straightforward decision for us. We wanted to be with her for Fourth of July and decided not to attend. This change was the first sign that things were changing in our relationships and identity.

In the first 12 to 18 months after she was born, we received invitations and were included in all parties with our LGBTQ friends. As time progressed, we saw on social media that events were happening and we were no longer invited. We surmised that they knew that we would probably say no, so they just stopped asking us. This change stung on one level, yet we knew that we were doing the things that were important to us.

For both myself and Lorevic, we struggled with this change in our communities and identities. We still strongly identified as gay men, which became secondary to our status as parents. We both had worked hard to find self-acceptance and self-love as gay men. Our gay identities didn't come to us quickly, and it felt hard to let them go and identify more as parents.

We found ourselves socializing more with straight couples with children. We discovered that we had a lot more in common with them and we enjoyed the time together as parents. This situation opened a new world of friends to us. We were often the only gay couple invited, but we found that our sexual orientation didn't matter. On some level, it felt great to be identifying with people outside of sexuality. While sexuality is always part of ourselves and most situations, it no longer felt like the center of it. It felt like a new world of interests were opening up to us.

We tried to forge new relationships with same-sex couples. We attended social events organized by Our Family Coalition, a California organization that advances equity for LGBTQ families with children, in the hopes of creating new friendships, yet we encountered many more families with two women than with two men. We became incredibly close to a lesbian couple with two adopted children. We tried to make deeper friendships with other men with children, but it has been more elusive than we hoped. At IAC's annual Christmas party, we met another family with two dads and a son the same age as Kaitlyn. We hit it off right away and had lots in common with them. We all decided to connect for a play date and exchanged numbers. After the Christmas party, we were excited about the chance to create a new friendship with other gay dads. We called several times and they never returned our calls. We often felt like we were drifting between identities and didn't fit into either camp. While on one level, it felt good to forge our path and personality, it also felt a little lonely to not fit into either group.

In the previous three years, our careers had taken a back seat to our goal to become parents. We couldn't make significant job changes as we had no idea of when our daughter would arrive and the requirements of parenting and adoption. After our daughter's adoption finalization, we jumped back into our jobs and both pushed forward with our careers. It was during this time I decided to change companies, which was very disruptive to our family life. I had been coasting a while at work, putting most of my energy into our family efforts. After we both went back to work, we hired a nanny to come to our house to take care of our daughter. We both had demanding jobs and wanted the reliability of a nanny at home. We also felt a sense of guilt for leaving our daughter in the care of someone else. Lots of parents struggle with putting their children into day-care. We felt better about having a nanny come to our house because it meant our daughter would have more one-on-one attention. This individual care helped assuage our guilt. It also made our lives easier with no drop-offs or pick-ups and some help with chores.

During all of this transition, we were elated to hear about the change from the U.S. Supreme Court on marriage equality. On Friday, June 26, 2015, in a 5-4 decision, the Court held that the Fourteenth Amendment requires all states to grant same-sex marriages and recognize same-sex marriages granted in other states. It was a momentous day that many of us felt would never come in our lifetimes. Lorevic and I decided to go to San Francisco City Hall the next day, get our license, and legalize our marriage.

The atmosphere in City Hall was electric and packed with folks who wanted to get married as soon as possible. After we obtained our license and waited for our names to be called, Governor Gavin Newsom appeared with his daughter. We shared a very warm moment with him as our daughters played together. Jill arrived, rushing down to join us, and was the sole witness who took our picture as we exchanged our vows.

CHAPTER 19

EXPANDING OUR FAMILY

AFTER HANDLING ALL the change, we settled into a routine, and everything was going well with our family. We both wanted another child, but we weren't sure we wanted to deal with all the uncertainty and disruption again. Our careers were starting to accelerate. My husband was working as a senior manager at the money transfer giant, Paypal, in San Jose, and I was working as a senior manager at Genentech, a member of the Roche Group, which is a leading biotechnology company that discovers and commercializes medicines to treat patients with serious or life-threatening medical conditions, like cancer. Lorevic and I had gotten into a rhythm with each other, our daughter, our nanny, our families, and our friends. We had created a new normal for our family of three, and our day-to-day life had become predictable again. Our daughter was healthy and meeting all her milestones. She adjusted quickly to her new caretaker. My husband and I were starting to reconnect on a deeper level. The first one to two years as a parent are so demanding that we didn't have a lot of time to nurture our own relationship.

Things were starting to feel very comfortable again, so why would we want to take on the responsibility, chaos, and uncertainty of another adoption and child? But as we settled in as a family, we felt a sense of long-ing for another child. We both thought we had more love to give. We felt a sense of unbalance with three of us. Two adults and one child felt like too much adult energy and too much responsibility for one child to bear. We thought about our daughter's experience of adoption and not having someone in the family to have the same experience. We thought about the adventures of a child and the importance of sharing those experiences with a sibling. We were both the youngest of families of four children. We had gained so much from our interactions with our siblings, and we felt that it wouldn't be fair to our daughter to deny her a sibling.

Another factor that was pushing us to make a decision about our sec-ond child was the fact that Lorevic's 40th birthday was approaching and I was 47. We weren't getting any younger and it felt like we needed to act soon because the window was closing. With Kaitlyn, it took us about three years from thinking about a child to having her. We knew it would take a long time to adopt another child. We knew that as we settled into more comfort within our lives, we would be less motivated to feel uncomfort-able again. Kaitlyn was potty training and she was becoming more inde-pendent. We were starting to socialize again and had date nights together. My best friend, Jeff, was babysitting on a pretty regular basis so Lorevic and I could go to the movies and dinner. Every few months, we took Kaitlyn to Mama and Papa's (Lorevic's parents') house for an overnight. We went to San Francisco and stayed at a downtown hotel for a romantic getaway. We met friends for parties and late-night bar crawling in the Castro. The idea of diapers, feedings, and sleepless nights become less appealing as you get further away from them.

We talked to friends and family about our dilemma, and they provided a range of opinions. None of them helped us move forward with our deci-sion until we spoke with my friend Kathi, who is the mother of two adult children. She asked a simple yet powerful question, "Does your family feel complete now?" She explained to us that when she had her second child that it just felt right, and she knew that two children made the family complete for her and her husband. When she asked us that question, we couldn't answer definitely, which meant our family wasn't done being formed and someone was missing.

Once we had made this monumental decision to expand our family, we needed to think through the options for our second child. Our first child came to us through private, open adoption and we went back to IAC to discuss our second child. We found out that there were well over 400 families waiting for children, this was a 100% increase since we started with them in 2010. During our wait for Kaitlyn, Annie, our social worker, told us that many birth mothers prefer to place their children with families with no other children. She said that birth mothers felt more comfortable with adoption when their child was getting the love from two parents and not sharing that focus with another child. While we didn't have hard facts to support these stories, it intuitively made sense to us that birth mothers might feel this way. We were able to view all adoptive families on the portal, and there were almost none that had other children. Since there was a backlog of hundreds of families waiting for children, it felt like it might take significantly longer than the two years we waited for Kaitlyn.

There was another question that kept coming up for us—what about children in the foster system who needed a loving family? How could we help a child who was facing an even less certain future? How could we give back and support the neediest? Our faith in God and our ability to handle a child with more significant needs were part of the discernment process. We believed that God would bring us the child that was meant to be part of our lives either through the private or foster-to-adopt system. Kaitlyn came to us after 14 contacts with different women and she was meant to be part of our family. We knew that the child meant for us would come into our lives. Our faith kept us on this journey to build our family.

For our first child, we wanted an adoption that was the least risky, although there is always a risk with adoption. We couldn't imagine the possibility of losing our child and made our decision to alleviate the risk as much as possible. For private adoption, the rate of reclaim from adoptive parents is somewhere between 2 to 5%[10] versus the foster-to-adopt system, where the reunification rate is between 10 to 25%.[11] These statistics vary by state and adoption agency but provide a glimpse into the prevalence of not finalizing an adoption. The goal of the two types of adoption is very different. For our second child, we felt much more open to the riskier foster-to-adopt avenue because we already were parents.

We had become very close with Elana and Marlene, two moms who had recently gone through the adoption of their second child. Elana and Marlene were our closest queer and adoptive friends. They had adopted both of their children through Bay Area Family Formation, also known as BAFF, which places children through the Bay Area counties' foster-to-adopt programs. Their oldest child was one month older than Kaitlyn. We had experienced many of the same milestones together and had walked through many experiences together. Their first adoption through the foster-to-adopt system was straightforward and quick. Their second adoption was more complicated. They faced obstacles along the way and jumped through many hoops to complete their second adoption. While we were aware of some of their challenges, we were not walking in their shoes and didn't fully grasp the situation. Whenever we saw them, they seemed very optimistic about finalizing their second adoption despite their obstacles. From our vantage point, they didn't seem stressed or concerned about finalizing the second adoption. Perhaps we heard what we wanted or didn't hear about the pain and suffering they had experienced with their second adoption. When we got together with them, we saw these two amazing children and this family full of love. Their situation gave us a false sense of security about the reality that we would face with our second adoption.

---

[10] Wrixon, "Independent Adoption."
[11] Child Welfare Information Gateway, "Adoption."

An advantage of their experience with BAFF was that children were placed in their home shortly after they completed their required paperwork. In the case of their first child, they started the adoption process in 2011, one year after we started the process, and their daughter was placed with them within a few months of completing their paperwork. We waited two years for Kaitlyn, and it felt like a lifetime. Another essential part of our decision was the ability to adopt an infant. While the public information available about the foster-to-adopt system generally describes placing older children, Elana and Marlene were matched with infants. In general, Elana and Marlene had a very positive experience with BAFF and encouraged us to consider foster-to-adoption as an option.

As we considered the decision for the path for our second adoption, many of the things that were most important to us would be possible with the foster-to-adopt agency. After searching our hearts and heads, we decided to move forward with BAFF's foster-to-adopt program for our second child.

As part of BAFF approval process, we were required to attend a one-day, eight-hour training and participate in subsequent workshops with guest speakers. Since we were already parents, we didn't see the need to complete these workshops, but BAFF required it of all prospective parents regardless of parental status. These trainings contained information for first-time parents going through the adoption process, information about transracial adoptions and bonding with children who have experienced trauma in their lives. At the time, this information did not seem relevant. In hindsight, we learned a lot about dysregulation and trauma that would be helpful in the future.

The process to become a foster-to-adopt parent was extensive with a total of 34 independent steps. These steps varied in complexity and time to complete. For example, there was a 16-page questionnaire about every aspect of our lives. BAFF required things like two years of tax returns, background checks, letters of recommendations, and CPR and first aid certification. The home study consisted of multiple visits to our home over six months in 2015 and the completion of the foster home inspection report. BAFF assigned a home study social worker, Martha, who was finishing her master's degree, to complete our home study. Martha came to our house every month to ask a series of personal questions about our backgrounds and parenting, such as how much we drank, if we ever did drugs, if we ever experienced physical or sexual abuse, and on and on. Her line of questions was very intrusive, and it felt almost a little inappropriate. She inspected every room in our house, asked to look inside our cabinets and drawers, and went outside of our house to inspect our yard. At one point, she instructed us to clean our windows as a requirement from the state. When Martha completed our home study, we never interacted with her again. The process of getting certified to become a foster-to-adopt parent was more rigorous than our experience with IAC, which required one home visit. We started the process with BAFF in January 2015 and we were approved to "go live" in the system in November 2015, 11 months later. At end of this period, we were assigned a placement social worker named Joy. We felt relieved to have completed the administrative process and were now waiting for our second child come into our lives.

Over the next couple of months, we were focused on celebrating Thanksgiving and preparing for Christmas with a toddler. After BAFF approved us, we didn't hear anything from Joy over the next couple of months. From our experience with IAC, we heard from our placement social worker every month with an update on the number of contacts during the month. From November 2015 to January 2016, we didn't hear anything from Joy. Our friends, Elana and Marlene, encouraged us to be more assertive and proactive with the agency and Joy.

Every month, social workers from the Bay Area counties share with the various adoption agencies the profiles of the children in the county foster system and the adoption agencies share the profiles of the prospective adoptive families. Then, the social worker representing each foster child and the social worker for the prospective adoptive parents discuss whether or not there is a good fit for the needs of the child and the adoptive parents. In late January, we found out that BAFF had not actively been sharing our profile with the Bay Area county social workers. Despite being approved for adoption, none of the county social workers could consider us for the children in their care. We were so ready for our second child and were hoping that it wouldn't take two years, as it did with Kaitlyn. We felt BAFF had dropped the ball on putting us in the pool of prospective parents and we were frustrated with this oversight. After finding this out, we became much more proactive. We began to check in with Joy every couple of weeks to determine our status and to keep our family top of mind for them. While we realized that there were many factors outside of our control, we wanted to encourage BAFF along the way.

CHAPTER 20

OUR SON ARRIVES

W E WALKED INTO the journey of adopting our second child somewhat ignorant of the trials and tribulations of the foster-to-adopt system. While the journey was challenging to finalize our daughter's adoption, it pales in comparison to our son. For our daughter's approval, we were not dealing directly with a county social services agency in the decision-making process. Mainly, it was a decision between us and Lyla and Justin with the assistance of IAC and lawyers to make sure that the legal requirements were met. With the foster-to-adopt system, the decision-makers were a large group of agencies and people including the Department of Social Services (DSS), the Unified Family Court of the Superior Court, BAFF, the child's court-appointed attorney, and a wide network of social workers, advocates, and health care professionals. Fate, resilience, patience, time and perseverance would be major factors in the long, drawn-out process.

Once we decided to move forward with our second adoption, we relied on our faith to help guide us on the journey and, as parishioners at Most Holy Redeemer Church in the Castro, we relied on our community to help us through the process. In hindsight, if we had better understood the risks associated with the foster-to-adopt system, we would have gone into the process better prepared for the emotional toll. Ignorance is bliss in many cases, and I think that was the case for us. It had been years since we attended the Alameda County foster-to-adopt workshop, and we had forgotten the guidance of the Alameda County social worker. We had also seen Elana and Marlene's positive experience and those of others who had gone through the foster-to-adopt through BAFF.

The foster-to-adopt system in California is not for the faint of heart. It is a system that advances the paths of both birth parents and foster parents in tandem. It's called concurrent planning. We learned about it in BAFF's required training to be approved for the adoption process through the foster system. While taking this training, we focused on the "adopt" portion of the foster-to-adopt. We viewed the "foster" part of the description as a steppingstone to the adoption. We didn't consider that it was possible the adoption wouldn't happen. The reality of the system was starkly different. Social services' primary goal is the safety, permanency, and well-being of children and, whenever possible, the reunification of biological parents with their biological children. Each county in California interprets its mission slightly differently based on the community and cultural aspects of that county.

At the time, our daughter was three-and-a-half years old. She was going to day-care Monday through Friday and taking swimming and hula lessons on the weekend. Lorevic and I were both working 40 to 50 hours a week. I was a senior marketing manager supporting a sales team on the East Coast. I was traveling every four to six weeks for work and away from home for several days. Our lives were incredibly busy and yet we knew our family wasn't complete. In our quest to adopt our second child, we faced dissonance in the logical aspects of the process and the reality of our feelings. We began thinking through the steps and requirements of the adoption since we had done it all before. We didn't understand the complicated feelings until we faced the prospect of losing our beloved foster son. It's a system of no control and all the responsibility, probably a good training ground for parenting. We had to dig deep in our souls during the tough times to handle the trauma of the process.

Once we decided to adopt another child, it took about 15 months from our first interaction with BAFF until we received the call for placement of a child in our home. In March 2016, I received the call that there was a five-month-old boy named Matthew who was at the UCSF Benioff Children's Hospital in Mission Bay with an acute injury, other health issues, and in need of a stable family. Our placement social worker, Joy, had limited information about Matthew's well-being, and she indicated that there was an urgency to find a family for him. It was so exciting and scary at the same time. Our gut told us to move forward quickly, and we also wanted additional information to help understand the bigger picture of the overall health of the child.

During our process to be certified as foster-to-adopt parents, we went through a long questionnaire on what type of child we would be willing to adopt. As a transracial family, we were open to any race, ethnicity, and gender. Lorevic and I are both able-bodied and had no experience with physical disabilities in our lives, so we knew there could be limitations on our ability to raise a child with physical disabilities. It was hard, but we had to be honest with ourselves for this process and felt that if there was a choice, we believed that a child with physical disabilities deserved parents who were experienced and better equipped to provide the necessary support. So, we noted that we preferred an infant or toddler without physical disabilities. We also didn't want twins because we just didn't think we could manage two infants at the same time.

We were open to drug and alcohol exposure, as many drugs have an acute impact on children and wash out of the body over time. We imagined that we could handle short-term health challenges with drug-related withdrawal but could not handle more long-term disabilities. The impact of alcohol exposure is more difficult to understand at birth and may show up later in life. But since alcohol use is so common, we were concerned that if we eliminated anyone who had consumed alcohol during pregnancy that the pool of potential birth mothers would be too small. While we were uneasy about the long-term effects of alcohol exposure, we decided to accept this risk in our selection process.

When we received the call about Matthew, we were so excited about the prospect of meeting him. We had completed the list of preferences so long ago we didn't remember all the details. We were unnerved by the situation because the information about Matthew was so vague and non-specific. When Joy called us, she did not have access to any written information about Matthew. To make matters worse, DSS's social worker, Cindy, who was the case manager for Matthew, was on vacation and Joy couldn't speak with her. Joy needed to rely on secondhand information from Cindy's supervisor, who had a massive caseload for many other children. There was a lack of reliable information, which made us scared. During the ongoing process through the foster-to-adopt system, we learned how the mechanisms and technology were antiquated. The files of the children in the foster system were not in electronic format but instead physical paper files. In my opinion, the lack of accurate, trustworthy, and real-time information about children in the foster system is affecting the prospects of those children getting placed for adoption. I will save this rant for another time, but the lack of technology and modern systems are hurting these kids and needs to change.

From what little information we could gather, Matthew was in the hospital from an accident and was waiting for a family to take him home. As someone who worked in healthcare, I knew the hospital would have detailed information on his condition because they are required to monitor and capture this information for the care plan. The hospital could not share accurate information with us until we were taking custody. With all this swirling in our heads, we were excited to meet Matthew and get to know him.

Matthew had been living with a foster family for the last four months, and this family was trying to adopt him. Initially, they only wanted to be foster parents. They quickly changed their minds when they fell in love with him and started the process to become adoptive parents. The accident occurred while Matthew was in their care, and child protective services removed him immediately. Since the foster family first took custody of him, they didn't have any contact with the birth mother. Joy assured us the case would move toward adoption quickly. She explained that the court hadn't terminated parental rights yet, but since the birth parents weren't in the picture that it wasn't a significant issue.

Over the next 48 hours, we would quickly adjust to the possibility of an infant entering our lives. We were excited and scared of the unknown. This change was not only going to impact Lorevic and me, but we needed to consider the impact on Kaitlyn. For Kaitlyn's adoption, we didn't worry about the negative consequences of a failed adoption on anyone else other than ourselves. For this adoption, the stakes were much higher because we needed to protect her.

One of the fears we faced in the foster-to-adopt process was the prospect of losing a child after placement and the impact on Kaitlyn. We were worried about the loss she would feel after attaching with a potential sibling. We were concerned that she would be fearful about the stability of her placement with us if she saw another child leave our home and she might think that she could be taken away from us. We have always been very open with our daughter about her adoption since birth. We have normalized it as much as possible. We believe that honesty and transparency are key to building a trusting and bonded relationship with her. We also needed to protect her from unnecessary worry and fear about her placement. This predicament was a challenging part of this second, more risky adoption. We proceeded forward cautiously to ensure no significant disruption to our daughter.

We talked with Kaitlyn about the prospect of our family growing larger with the addition of a sibling. She was happy and looking forward to a sibling. We didn't talk often because we weren't sure when it would happen and we didn't have any idea about any of the details, so we kept the conversations with her very high level. After getting the call, we had to prepare her quickly for what was coming. We didn't share too much because we honestly didn't have a lot of information.

Another significant disruption to our lives was paternity leave and childcare. This time around, I was in the middle of several major projects with deadlines taking place over the next three months. These were big initiatives and difficult to hand off to someone else. On the other hand, my husband was in a lull and had more flexibility. This pattern of balancing our work lives with the demands of the family would play out for years as parents. We always felt lucky that we had each other to absorb these ups and downs.

As we drove to UCSF Benioff Children's Hospital to meet Matthew, we knew that our lives were about to be turned upside down again. We had almost no time to plan for the disruption, both emotionally and practically. Adoptions require a high level of faith, flexibility, and resilience with the many unknown factors that take place throughout the placement and adoption. We knew that uncertainty and lack of control would take over our lives, but we had no idea to what extent and the difficulty it would cause to us.

When we arrived at Mission Bay, we were giddy, scattered, and scared. In the last 48 hours, we received additional information from Joy about the circumstances of Matthew's life, and it was concerning. He was underweight for his age and received a diagnosis of "failure to thrive." It wasn't a precise diagnosis and it made things unclear. Was "failure to thrive" a genetic condition? Was it from exposure to drugs or alcohol? Or was it from his care after his birth? These were all questions that were swirling in our heads. We were trying to prepare for what care and treatment he would require. Initially, Joy communicated that he fractured his spine from his accident, which sounded severe. Before arriving at the hospital, she corrected that information and told us he had broken his arm and that it was recovering nicely. The lack of consistent and reliable information made us wonder what was going on with him.

We didn't know what we were walking into when we arrived. We knew that we wanted another child in our lives and we knew our hearts were open with love. Our faith told us that there was a preordained connection with Matthew. We knew that, for some reason, Matthew was chosen for us and we were chosen for him. In the previous 48 hours, we spent a lot of time considering the decision to meet him and we knew that meant we had to be very serious about adopting him. We prayed for guidance and searched our hearts for answers. We were ready to meet him.

After arriving at UCSF Benioff Children's Hospital, we checked in at security and got badges to proceed to the fourth floor where he was staying. UCSF Benioff Children's Hospital was less than one year old, and it looked more like a hotel than a hospital. The hallways were long and wide with nothing on the walls. It felt very empty and cold as we stepped into the elevator. When we arrived on the fourth-floor pediatric unit, we spent a lot of time talking with the nurses and the doctor who had been taking care of Matthew for the last five days. By all accounts, he was doing incredibly well. The nurses said that he was the sweetest little boy, and they did not want to see him leave the hospital. They had fallen in love with him and were very attached to him. They reassured us that he was getting the love and care that he needed to thrive. We spoke with the pediatrician for about 45 minutes to an hour about his medical condition, and she said that he could overcome his acute medical issues with proper love and care. She said the "failure to thrive" diagnosis in his case had nothing to do with a genetic predisposition but rather from the environments he had experienced from birth. She repeatedly said that he had no long-term medical issues. We were relieved and excited to meet him.

I remember it as clearly as yesterday. We walked down the long hallway to the room where he was staying and pushed this large, heavy metal door open. While the hospital felt cold and sterile, I held Lorevic's hand, which reminded me of the first time we touched and how scared I was to fall in love with him. I knew that our lives were about to change forever, and I felt excited and emotional. We walked into this huge hospital room with a large bed in the center of the room and a small baby rocker placed in the center of the bed. As soon as we opened the door, we saw Matthew with a smile from ear-to-ear and beautiful brown eyes. He looked up at us right away and our eyes locked immediately. We asked if we could hold him, and the nurse said yes. This time around, I was able to hold him first. It was pure joy as I picked him up and held his body for the first time. A cadre of social workers and nurses from the county, our agency, and the hospital surrounded us. It felt strange to have all these people there while we were holding our son for the first time. My gaze was glued to his face, and I couldn't take my eyes off this beautiful child. While activity was happening around me, it fell into the background as I held him and gazed into his eyes. His smile was infectious and he was oozing with love. Then, Lorevic held him for a long time. We fell in love immediately. He was perfect for us. We asked the social workers and nurses when we could take him home.

There was a ton of paperwork and guidance on what we needed to do medically. Lots of the information was not written down anywhere, and we were trying to pull everything together. There were so many things to do to get ready to take care of Matthew. It was all very overwhelming. For the moment, we focused on being present with him and savoring this slice of heaven.

Once we were able to head home, we were so excited to introduce Matthew to Kaitlyn. We arrived home and settled in with him. Then my husband went to pick up our daughter. We spoke with many parents who talked about the jealousy with the arrival of a second child. Our little girl was the center of our world, and that was all about to change. An infant needs so much attention, and our little guy needed more attention due to his circumstances. We didn't know what to expect with the transition, but we were excited for them to meet.

CHAPTER 21

BIRTH MOTHER RE-EMERGES

T HE DAY AFTER Matthew arrived home, we heard from Joy that his birth mother, Selena, had re-emerged from being out of the picture for several months and she wanted to see him. Birth parents automatically get six months of reunification services. Selena had not been engaged in the process before, but then came back into the picture and reengaged with services. Selena started her reunification services and was interested in trying to get healthy to find out if she could regain custody of Matthew. WHAT?! Cindy, DSS's social worker, assured us that because of the way Matthew came into the system that it would be unlikely that he could reunify with Selena. How did this happen? Two days ago, we were told that there was almost no chance of his birth mother regaining custody and now they were talking about visits with her. We were terrified.

At the time, we didn't fully understand what this all meant. After taking care of Matthew for only one day, we had opened our hearts and were already becoming attached to him. Since we received the call, there was no mention of the birth parents' involvement, and the adoption process seemed like it would require administrative hurdles but nothing more. With this news about the birth mother, we were stunned and scared to death.

We were in love with this addition to our family. The next year and a half would turn into a stressful and scary time for our family. We were determined to love Matthew with all our hearts and provide a safe and loving home for him to grow and prosper.

The next day was the beginning of our journey with Selena. As part of her re-entry into reunification services, she was now entitled to have supervised visits with Matthew. Joy told us repeatedly that in her more than 15 years of experience, many of the birth mothers cannot fulfill their reunification requirements and therefore do not reunite with their kids. She said that we should not worry because he would continue on the path to adoption with our family. Her reassurance made us feel a little better, but we were utterly unprepared for the next steps in the process and we were worried. We felt the instinct to protect him and we wanted to keep him safe.

We had our first visit with Selena at the DSS office, which lasted for three hours. Due to his injury, he was considered medically fragile and DSS required that the foster parents and social worker needed to be present during visits while he was healing. The first visit was incredibly awkward and hard for all of us. Since Matthew had just arrived in our home, we were getting to know him and his way of being. We were still learning his sounds and cries, his movements and discomforts, and how to feed him and care for him. During the visit, we shared feeding and changing diapers with Selena. It felt entirely unsettling to be under Selena's and Joy's microscope while we tried to get to know Matthew. We sensed her discomfort, as well.

After this visit, we picked up Kaitlyn and spent the rest of the weekend bonding as a family and taking care of Matthew. This first weekend together was so joyous and chaotic as we quickly adapted to having a second child. Not only was it our first weekend with Matthew, but it was also Easter Sunday. Easter holds a special place in our hearts because it was when Kaitlyn came into our lives four years earlier. We felt joy for the gift of his life into our family and we felt blessed that we came together as a family. On Easter Sunday, we went to Most Holy Redeemer to celebrate

Easter and introduced Matthew to our church community. Father Matt was so excited to meet Matthew and offered his prayer and support for our journey toward adoption. Father Matt informed us that the name Matthew means "Gift from God," which felt so fitting for our son. Father Matt would be an essential part of our support system in our ongoing battle to adopt Matthew. He would provide Lorevic and me with hope and prayers as we struggled with the uncertainty of the future.

We had a fantastic weekend bonding together as a family; there was also the stress of bringing a new member of the family into our house. Our daughter didn't have a lot of time to prepare for the change in her life. While she loved Matthew from the minute she met him, she had a significant adjustment to not being an only child. Matthew came into our home one month before Kaitlyn turned four. She had grown used to being the center of attention and our lives. We had kept lots of baby paraphernalia from our daughter, which was helpful, but we had given a lot of things away when we moved and needed all of the basics again. It was a hectic weekend on all fronts. The day after Easter, I went back to work, and my husband began his paternity leave for the next three months.

When Matthew came into our lives, he had been through a lot. His transition into our family was not smooth. He was dysregulated from the many changes and trauma in his early life. Dysregulation for a child means their emotional response to situations don't correspond with the situation or setting. He was scared and uneasy being with us at first. He was super sensitive to sound and didn't want to sleep. It took us 30 to 45 minutes to get him to fall asleep. Once we thought he was sleeping, we would put him into his bassinet, the slightest move would awaken him, and he would begin to cry again. The cry would turn into a shriek, and we ran back into sooth him. Unlike Kaitlyn, he would cry and he wouldn't be able to soothe himself back to sleep. With Matthew, his cries had a sound of distress and pain, unlike we had experienced before. Once we were able to get him to go to sleep, he wouldn't stay asleep for long. He woke up frequently crying and scared. With our daughter, when she awoke during the night, it usually was attributed to hunger. With Matthew, when he woke we would try to feed him, but he didn't want the bottle. He needed to be held tightly to calm his body down. We attempted to swaddle him to calm his nervous system down, but he responded much better to the human touch.

During the daytime hours, he cried frequently and was very difficult to soothe. He needed a lot of physical touch and reassurance. Thank God for my husband and his patience. He took on the brunt of Matthew's care in the first three month since I was working. Lorevic was able to be with Matthew during his discomfort, and he was unaffected by his cries and pain. His calm and patient demeanor brought us through a very turbulent time.

Within the first couple of weeks of placement in our family, we met with Matthew's court-appointed lawyer, Sherine, who was responsible for ensuring his safety and protection. Sherine had the sole responsibility of determining what was best for Matthew in the long run and making recommendations to the judge for his long-term placement plan. She was the impartial third party that was not interested in our needs or the birth mother's needs. She focused solely on making the best decision for Matthew. When we met her, we didn't fully understand her role and her power. We had met so many different people in the last few weeks, and we didn't understand who was most important for the adoption process. As we prepared for our first meeting with her, we cleaned like crazy and wanted to make our home look like the perfect place to raise a child.

When she arrived at our home, Sherine walked into the door with elegance and energy that filled the room with confidence and determination. She was a strikingly beautiful woman with long brown hair and olive skin who looked like she belonged on the Paris Fashion Runway instead of driving her three kids around in a mini-van. While she was lovely, she was detached and unruffled by the situation. I was intimidated by her and kept looking at the clock to figure out when she would leave. Unlike many of the other professionals we encountered, who mostly had questionnaires and forms, she had the intention of looking inside our hearts and souls to figure out who we were. We had a cordial and informative discussion about the process and expectations. She never expressed any indication whether she thought Matthew would be better served in our care. She was very much eyeing us over and getting to know us. After she left, I took a deep breath and felt exhausted.

As gay dads, we were always conscious that not everyone is supportive of queer parents. While there were no outward signs of bias from Sherine or anyone else responsible for Matthew, we often wondered if our status as a same-sex couple had any impact on their decision to consider us to be fit as parents. This question popped up along the way and, in the end, I don't think this mattered at all. We were lucky to live in an area where our status as an LGBTQ couple didn't matter. In other parts of the country and world, this discrimination is real and hurting foster children and queer people.

Over the next several months, we would get an indoctrination in the ins-and-outs of the dependency court. In short order, the court order required twice weekly two-hour supervised visits with Selena until the next hearing. This requirement allowed Selena the time to participate in the reunification services to address the issues that brought Matthew into the dependency court system. California law provides six months of reunification services for a parent of a child under three. The court can extend this time to 12 months and, rarely, 18 months for a number of reasons. After reunification services are terminated, a .26 hearing is set 120 days later with a recommendation by DSS for a determination of the permanency plan. During the .26 hearing, DDS makes a recommendation to the court for a permanent plan, including adoption, legal guardianship, or long-term foster care in order of legal preference.

Lorevic quickly settled into a routine of visits every Tuesday and Thursday. Initially, he was required to stay for the appointments, and then he was able to leave Matthew with his birth mother and a social worker for a couple of hours. As any new parent knows, the demands of taking care of an infant are exhausting and trying. This two-hour break allowed us to have a short break to take care of ourselves and get some errands and personal things done. The drop-offs were always a little unnerving. There was always a social worker present and we would leave Matthew directly with Selena.

CHAPTER 22

INCOMPLETE FAMILY SEARCH

WHEN CINDY, THE DSS social worker, first contacted us about Matthew's placement in our home, she told us that DSS had completed the family search and she explained that the agency had done an extensive search to determine if there were any blood relatives interested in adopting Matthew. During the search, they didn't find any family members and he was available for adoption by a non-relative. This milestone is important because this removes a key barrier in the eyes of the law for adoption. While we were aware of Selena wanting to regain custody, there were no other relatives who were trying to adopt him.

One month after Matthew was in our home, I received a text message from Joy, our placement social worker, with a request for a meeting within a few hours. I was at my office, preparing to lead a team meeting for an important project. My husband was home with Matthew. I asked Joy if Lorevic could meet alone with her, but she requested that I come back to the house. My heart sank, and I was frantic. I left the office immediately to find out what was happening.

I raced home. Lorevic and I were both anxious to hear what was going on. We had become so attached to Matthew, and we were terrified about something that might take him away from us. When Joy arrived, we were on the edge of our seats, and we jumped right into the conversation. She reiterated that no relatives were stepping forward to adopt Matthew, but there was another family that might be interested in adopting him. The adoptive parents of one of his siblings had surfaced and they were interested in meeting Matthew. Joy said the courts are always interested in placing siblings together in the same home, and she added that if his sibling's adoptive parents wanted to adopt him they would have the right. Both Joy and Cindy told us to schedule a meeting with Matthew's brother's family quickly. After Joy left, we looked at each other with a sigh of relief that he wasn't being taken away immediately.

When I was preparing for the call with Amelia, the adoptive mother, I had a knot in the pit of my stomach. I had no idea of what questions she would ask or what were her expectations. I ran through a series of potential subjects in my head for days and tried to think through the best answers. After going through all the possible questions, I was afraid that the parents would want Matthew to become part of their family. We also feared that these parents would be homophobic and want Matthew raised by a mother and father versus our family of Papa and Daddy. This call reminded me of the multiple phone calls we had with expectant mothers where we were stepping into a high stress, high-risk situation without any idea of what to expect. In these situations, with pregnant mothers, we talked through the scenarios to prepare and role-played the conversation. We wanted to communicate our real intentions thoughtfully and transparently. These interactions were nerve-wracking, and we didn't want our nerves to cloud our plans. Even with all of our preparations, we always came back to our gut instincts, core beliefs, and inner voice. These interactions made us think hard about who we were and what were our feelings. This call with Amelia was no different.

A few days later, I called Amelia and we talked about Selena's situation, our children, our families, our backgrounds, and how adoption had created our families. I remember feeling like I had gone into a cave and had blocked the rest of the world out to give this mom 200% of my concentration. As a parent, sometimes it's hard to focus so intently as you are always listening for your kids and making sure they are safe. For this call, it felt like time had stopped, and she and I were the only people on the planet. At the end of the call, I felt exhausted and happy. She was a kind person concerned about Matthew's well-being over her own needs or some connection to biology. While Selena was pregnant with Matthew, Amelia and her family had lunch with Selena and Matthew's birth father, and they felt connected to Matthew. Amelia and her husband were open, inclusive people and indifferent about our family with two dads. Their primary concern was the children. They had another child adopted from a different birth family and, like our family, blood connections were not essential to creating a family. My anxiety had turned into excitement and anticipation for meeting them. While I worried they might want to adopt Matthew once they saw how adorable and sweet he was, I knew that this family would be part of our lives forever.

A couple of weeks later, we agreed to meet at our house for a play-date with the kids. Lorevic and I wanted to make an excellent first impression and spent a fair amount of time cleaning the house and getting ready with snacks and toys. When they arrived at the house, I was nervous and excited. I was looking forward to getting to know more about Matthew's birth family and his brother. Amelia had an open adoption agreement with Selena and spent time with her before their son was born and after they adopted him. I was looking forward to seeing how Matthew and his brother would react to each other. We wanted to create a strong bond with them.

Research shows that adopted kids who have more transparency and openness about their adoption are better adjusted and have a greater sense of their identity than those who don't.[12] We fully supported all aspects of open adoption. Despite the difficult conversations with our kids about the reasons for their adoptions and the challenges of explaining our family to

---

[12] Grotevant et al., "Contact."

other people, we make every effort to be fully open with our kids. This play-date with Matthew's brother felt like a tryout of sorts. We felt like they were assessing us as parents and, if we didn't perform well, that they could request to adopt him. This playdate was unnerving. We proceeded with trepidation, but once we all met, all the worry and concern faded away. We immediately felt connected, like extended lost relatives. All of the parents focused on doing what was best for Matthew. If that meant reunification with his biological brother, then we would support it. This meeting with his biological brother's family made us very excited about the prospect of having connections to his past, which would result in better relationships for him in the future. The family spent a couple of hours with us. While it was incredibly hectic with four kids running around and playing, we were able to talk to each other in-depth about hopes and dreams for our kids and families. We talked about how we would connect as an extended family to fully support the relationships with the biological families. At the end of the playdate, we all embraced and talked about getting together again soon.

A few days later, we received a phone call from Amelia that she wanted us to move forward with adopting Matthew. They loved meeting him and fell in love with us as a family. We breathed a massive sigh of relief that Matthew would be staying in our family, where he was meant to be, and we had overcome another hurdle in the adoption process.

Over the next couple of months, we fell into a routine as a family. We wanted to create a secure, stable environment for Matthew. I avoided business travel to be at home with Matthew and the rest of the family. Despite the busyness at work, I didn't feel the stress of parenting because Lorevic was handling the majority of the responsibilities. He settled into a routine with meetings with Selena. She was doing well in her program, and she was excited about her visits with Matthew. We were happy for her progress toward a healthy lifestyle and scared that her success would harm our adoption prospects.

Matthew arrived in our home with some acute health challenges, and it was unclear on the long-term impact on his health and well-being. In the first few months, we had frequent doctor visits. With each new doctor visit, we would leave feeling excited as his health was improving by leaps and bounds. He was eating frequently and gaining wait, growing stronger, and getting healthier with each passing day. While the doctor visits and medical requirements were daunting, we met kind, loving, and dedicated health care professionals who were giving our little boy love and gave us so much hope about the world.

As Lorevic's paternity leave came to an end, I began to prepare for the time at home with Matthew, which coincided with the summer. I was excited to spend more time with him and also take a break from work. While juggling work and parenting one child was difficult, the work of two kids and two jobs seemed impossible when dealing with a child who needed so much care and doctor visits. When I stopped working, I quickly jumped into full-time parenting and homemaking.

While Lorevic was good at building a relationship with Selena, I had a much harder time connecting with her. Lorevic was up to date on the trends and connected with the younger generation. He can compartmentalize different aspects of his life and remain calm amid incredible stress. It was hard for me to make small talk with her and I felt so protective of Matthew. I was full of fear about losing him and she represented that threat to me. It was tough for me to be lighthearted with her and not consider the potential impact on Matthew and our lives. I felt most uncomfortable with the drop-offs and pick-ups with Selena and the social worker. Matthew enjoyed his visits with her, which happened smack in the middle of his morning and afternoon naps. He was always in a good mood and happy to see her. Matthew loves people and loved connecting with his birth mother.

A difficult aspect of being a foster parent working with a social services system is the strict restrictions on who can babysit a foster child. DSS requires that anyone responsible for taking care of a foster child must receive background checks and the department's approval. This rule is great for the protection of the child but very cumbersome for family members or friends who want to babysit occasionally. With that said, we didn't get anyone else to watch Matthew during this period. The entire responsibility of taking care of Matthew fell on us, and it was exhausting due to the stress related to the adoption. DSS also required that any time you travel outside the county you get permission through the completion of an approval form. While the requirements were simple, the act of getting authorization brought us back to this feeling of having no control.

During the summer of 2016, everything was moving along without much activity with Sherine, Cindy, and Joy. The number of months were passing that Matthew was in our care, and we were starting to feel more confident in our prospects of adopting him. While Selena was doing very well in her program, Cindy and Joy made us feel sure that things were moving toward adoption. Cindy was supposed to come to our home every month for a wellness check on Matthew, which she didn't do. Instead, she met those requirements during Selena's visits at the DSS office.

Another aspect of the foster-to-adopt process that is challenging is that the majority of the time, things are moving along generally with limited interactions with social workers and the human services department. You are mostly doing the work of parenting like any other parents. You forget that your foster child is "not your child" and you love them like they are yours forever. Then, there are episodes when you need to be on high alert, focused on the details of paperwork, process, court dates, and vital information from the attorneys, social workers, etc. Those periods of normalcy give you a false sense of security.

In late July 2016, Cindy came for her first visit to our home. We had a strong relationship with her and she was supportive of the adoption. During our meeting with her, we learned that she was a lesbian mom raising an adopted daughter. She was sympathetic to our journey and she gave us hope as someone on the other side of the process. Her daughter was in her twenties, and it was nice to hear her experiences along the way. During this meeting, she shared that she was working on her report for the court for a recommendation to terminate Selena's reunification services. The termination of reunification services was a crucial milestone in the road to adoption. Even though Selena was doing well, Cindy didn't believe that Selena should regain custody. She had reviewed her recommendation with her supervisor, who was also supportive of our adoption of Matthew.

After this meeting, we felt like we had reached the top of Mount Everest and we were beginning the descent to the base. We were relieved and felt the stress of uncertainty melt away. We had been working closely with all of the people responsible for the well-being of our child and we felt like our efforts were finally paying off. With this news, we planned a trip to Chicago to introduce Matthew to my family, and we also planned a trip to Southern California. We were so excited to start living life again without fear of losing Matthew hanging over us.

CHAPTER 23

REUNIFICATION SERVICES EXTENDED

O N A FRIDAY afternoon, we left work early and piled into our SUV for our road trip to Ventura County. On Saturday morning, we headed over to Katie and Seth's house for a pool party. We felt on top of the world as we felt like we had moved past our biggest obstacle to adoption of Matthew. We had a quintessential Southern California day in the sun. About 4 p.m., we received an email from Sherine that rocked our world. Sherine notified us that DSS had changed their recommendation. The department decided to provide Selena another six months of reunification services. We also learned that Cindy, the DSS social worker, suddenly went on medical leave and we were assigned a new social worker, Diego. The email was minimal and there was no information about the justification for the change. It was the weekend, so no one from DSS was answering their phones. We panicked and were frenzied. We called Sherine immediately. She didn't answer on the first attempt. We eventually got through to her and she didn't have any additional information. She was confused by the change in recommendation but couldn't provide any reassurance. Was it something that we had done that the department had lost confidence in us as prospective parents? Or was the department more confident in Selena's capability and want to give her more time to get healthy?

Thank God for our friends. They watched the kids as we were holed up in a room, processing our emotions, and doing research on the internet about lawyers to consult. DSS does not like foster parents to have their own lawyer. Getting a lawyer puts you in an adversarial position with DSS. Matthew had been in our care for five months, and the thought of losing him made us crazy. I wanted to crawl out of my skin and hide in a corner. I was so scared that he would leave our lives and our family would shatter. The weekend getaway quickly turned into panic and the change in the recommendation felt like a message of something more profound.

When we returned home, my panic turned into an anxious dread where I felt like a puppet who was completely out of control of my movements and dependent on others to move forward. The next six weeks would turn from a time of joy and bonding to torturous thoughts about what was the "right" move for us to save our family. Matthew was doing much better and his first birthday was approaching. We were thrilled to watch him hit this milestone, but we were torn up inside about our family coming apart. When we returned from L.A., we spoke with Cindy's supervisor who would not give us details about her departure. She only provided general information about why they were changing their recommendation. DSS had changed its guidance because Selena was doing better and deserved additional time to get fully healthy.

This change seemed totally out of sync with everything else we had heard for the last five months from Joy and Cindy. Something did not seem right about this change in recommendation, but we couldn't get a straight answer. Joy was very involved in Matthew's placement with us, but when push came to shove, she was hesitant to advocate more for us with DSS. From this situation, we realized that DSS held more power and influence over Matthew's care and BAFF had more of an administrative role. Joy told us for months that we didn't need to worry about the adoption moving forward. But things had taken a drastic step backward, and no one seemed to know why. We wanted answers. Matthew's future was on the line, and everyone else seemed super casual about this change.

We didn't feel like we were getting the advocacy we needed from Joy or BAFF. So, we decided to elevate our concerns to her manager to get additional information about what the agency could be doing to protect our beloved son. We scheduled a meeting with Joy, her manager, Lorevic, and myself. This meeting felt like a do-or-die situation, where we would get a commitment from BAFF to do more for our son and our family. We were looking for action from the agency to advocate for us. We spent a lot of time on the call discussing the history and the current situation. Joy and her manager reminded us that when we went through our training to become foster-to-adopt parents that they informed us that 10 to 25% of kids are returned to their birth families. She said we signed an agreement that we understood the risk of return and agreed to the terms of the contract. They said this with an indifferent tone, and hearing these words felt like a gut punch. During the training and for the last five months, they had downplayed this risk, and Joy told us repeatedly that in our case, it was incredibly unlikely that this would happen. This meeting with Joy and her manager felt like a complete 180-degree change and they reiterated that we had zero legal standing in this situation. Lorevic and I were in shock and total dismay. How was it possible that we became Matthew's protectors and guardians without recourse? They advised us not to get a lawyer and told us that it would hurt our case to have a lawyer. They told us to go back home, continue to treat Matthew like our son, and wait for more time to pass. After this meeting, we realized that most of the power and decision-making did not reside with BAFF and we needed to focus our energy on Diego, our new DSS social worker.

Selena continued to do well in her rehabilitation program and meeting all of her commitments mandated by the court. Diego started to talk about more extended visits for Matthew and the possibility of him doing overnights with Selena. This scenario sounded like a big step toward reunification. We were in shock and reeling at the possibility of Matthew leaving us. I recall dropping him off for visits with Selena. I would get back into my car, drive around the block, park my car, and break down in tears. I cried and cried and cried. I was inconsolable, lost, and felt out of control. After breaking down, I picked myself up, stopped thinking about my pain, and focused on helping Matthew. My faith in what was best for him helped pick me up and move forward.

Lorevic and I went against the advice of BAFF and hired an attorney, Daniel, who had expertise in foster-to-adopt cases. We reached out to him confidentially and did not inform anyone. We needed to better understand from a completely unbiased third party what we could do to save our family. I scheduled an appointment and frantically prepared questions for our meeting. On the day of the meeting, Lorevic had something come up at work and couldn't come in person. My friend, Jill, volunteered to go to the meeting with us so she could help watch Matthew while we discussed our situation with the attorney. She chased our energetic boy up and down four flights of stairs several times while we met with Daniel.

Daniel had been a temporary judge on the dependency court and knew many of the decision-makers at the Unified Family Court of the Superior Court and DSS. He mostly reinforced the message that we had heard from BAFF that we had no rights and the situation lay in the hands of the courts at this point. Daniel stated that the courts do not like to move children after six months of placement with a foster family, which could have harmful effects on the bonding the child had done with the foster family. We were one month short of Matthew being in our care for six months. This time requirement gave us a sliver of hope. We felt like time was on our side, as Matthew would continue to be in our care for at least another six months. This extension also was terrifying—that he might be in our care for over one year and then be removed. Daniel also suggested that the court might consider a bonding evaluation as proof that Matthew was more bonded with us than his birth mother. The bonding evaluation determines the quality of the child's attachment to birth and foster parents to understand who fills the position of the most significant importance in a child's emotional life. At this point, we were grasping at straws and thinking about any way to keep Matthew in our family.

We left that meeting feeling like our lives were in the hands of fate and that there was nothing we could do to influence the court or process. All we needed to do was to continue to love and care for Matthew despite the uncertainty. It was so easy to love him, yet incredibly hard not to hold back in fear. Both Lorevic and I had built our individual and collective lives by taking actions to make a change. In this situation, we could do NOTHING to change the circumstances that were paralyzing to us. We had to dig deep inside ourselves and look to God for some peace of mind. I relied heavily on my friends and my family to help me manage through the situation. I was in contact with Elana almost every other day. She was sympathetic to our circumstances and she understood my dread. I prayed a lot. I asked for the prayers of Father Matt, our church community, family, friends, and co-workers.

With Cindy on medical leave, it felt like we were starting over with the process. When we first learned of Cindy's absence, we knew nothing about Diego, the new DSS social worker. We quickly learned that he was highly respected with excellent references which made us hopeful about moving forward. Diego needed to evaluate us and our application to become parents independently. After the sudden change in recommendation from DSS, we didn't know what to expect from Diego. Would he be looking for areas of deficiency in us as parents? What was his directive from the higher-ups who had changed their recommendation? In the midst of all this, we scheduled a home visit with him to meet Matthew and our family. Unlike Cindy, Diego was very interested in coming into our home and seeing Matthew's environment. We made the house look pristine and got Matthew's room looking great for the first visit. When Diego arrived, he was straight-laced and formal. He was significantly younger than Cindy and seemed very by-the-book. We met with him for 30 minutes, and he didn't provide any additional detail on what happened. He said he needed to comply with all requirements and assess the situation, and he would be getting back to us.

We felt that something fishy was happening with Cindy's sudden departure, and there was a blackout of information about what was happening with DSS. Neither Diego nor Sherine could provide additional insights into what was happening behind the scenes. This lack of information didn't help calm our worries.

In the midst of all of this, we were going to Chicago for vacation. We had submitted our vacation form and were awaiting approval. We had been completely transparent about our planned vacation, and everyone seemed on board with the plan, but they were incredibly slow to return the completed travel form. With all the changes and uncertainty, it was unnerving that the form wasn't complete. After making several phone calls and urging people, we finally received our approved travel form about 12 hours before our flight.

The vacation was a needed break from the weekly visits and the stress of the previous few weeks. We arrived in Chicago and stayed with my mom. We enjoyed a fun and active vacation, seeing relatives and introducing Matthew to lots of family members. The week was uneventful, and it was nice to not have any activity with Selena, Diego, Joy, or Sherine. This trip was the first time Matthew had left the state and flown on an airplane. It felt like a critical milestone in our journey to adopt him.

When we returned home, we prepared for the next week and returning to the routine of biweekly visits with Selena. We were also preparing for the upcoming court date for the hearing about reunification services. I felt utterly unsettled with all the changes and the court date. I was in the process of returning to work in a few weeks. Lorevic and I were working to find childcare for Matthew and trying to figure out how we were going to navigate biweekly visits with Selena and both of us working. Since the biweekly visits were in a supervised location 10 miles away from home, Matthew had to be transported to see Selena. Lorevic and I weren't sure how we were going to break away from work for four hours twice per week. We discussed this challenge with Diego and he advised us that DSS agreed to provide transportation back and forth for visits. This situation made me very nervous due to the long distance. Matthew was less than one-year-old and I was apprehensive about him getting picked up every Tuesday and Thursday by a different driver and how he would handle the situation. Children between the ages of seven to 18 months go through the phase of "stranger danger," and I worried about Matthew getting scared with the lack of continuity of drivers and caretakers. We were anticipating disruption and uncertainty with the start of day-care. Then, for him to have to leave every other day with a stranger—it just seemed like too much.

When Monday rolled around, we all started back into our routines. Lorevic jumped back into work, Kaitlyn returned to day-care, and Matthew and I restarted our pattern of breakfast, nap, playing, lunch, nap, and snuggling. It had been a few weeks since our world turned upside down with the news from social services. We felt like we were walking on shaking ground but still moving forward. During these weeks, I reflected on our time with Matthew and our journey together. I tried to think about the benefit to Matthew from our care even if he left our home. I thought about the gifts of love, safety, security, and growth that we had given him and how these gifts would stay with him forever. If it was beneficial for Matthew to return to Selena, then the time he spent in our family would serve him for the rest of his life. I envisioned seeing him as a teenager, excelling in his life, and thinking that we had played a little part in helping him become this well-adjusted, happy kid. In the midst of all of my fears and worry, these thoughts gave me a little solace and a sense of distant happiness. On the other hand, I thought about how I would fall apart with the loss, which seemed daunting and consuming.

CHAPTER 24

MANDATORY VISIT MISSED

T HE NEXT DAY, we prepared for Matthew's visit with Selena. I put together his diaper bag with everything needed for his care and added his lunch. It had been nice to have a break from the routine and the feelings that came up with them. We drove to the supervised location in the halfway house as usual. I arrived and parked the car and pulled out his car seat to carry him to his visit. I loaded up the diaper bag and slung it around my shoulder. I headed to the drop-off location where I met with Selena and a social worker in the past. I waited for a few minutes, and no one appeared. Then, I started to check my watch. Did I get the day or time wrong? Where was everyone? A woman emerged from the building and told me that Selena was not there. I inquired if I should wait for her to return or what I should do. I certainly didn't want to be responsible for missing a visit. I called Diego and Joy and couldn't get through to anyone. The regular social worker who supervised the visits was on vacation, and the temporary social worker didn't have any information. I finally picked him back up, returned to the car, and we drove home. I was stunned and numb, and I had no idea what to do. When I finally spoke with Joy, she was unaware of any problems and suggested Selena might have had a doctor appointment or something else. I knew it was not a good sign for her to miss a visit. No one seemed to have any information about her whereabouts, and no one provided clear direction for what to do next. I was worried about what happened to her. I was advised by Joy to continue with the regular biweekly visits.

For the next visit, I went back to the same location and again, Selena didn't emerge. I waited for 15 minutes and left. Later, we found out that she abandoned her mandated program and was in violation of the court order. While we were very concerned about her well-being, we were relieved that this change would mean more time with Matthew.

The next day, we were scheduled to meet with Sherine to discuss the upcoming court date. We had multiple communication with her since the change in recommendation from DSS, but most of the conversation was process-driven. We didn't get any information in our phone and email interactions about what she thought about our prospects of adopting Matthew.

Lorevic decided to work from home that day to be available to meet with Sherine. Matthew and I had left to take Kaitlyn to school. When we returned, I heard yelling coming from our home office, which was completely uncharacteristic of Lorevic. At first, I didn't pay attention to the shouting. I figured it was something work-related and none of my business. After a couple of minutes of the yelling continuing, I knocked on the door and entered the room. He muted the phone and told me that it was Selena. The conversation went on for over an hour, and she expressed anger, sadness, despair, and conviction to get Matthew back. She also expressed gratitude to us for caring for him. She was in so much pain. During the call, Lorevic took copious notes with quotations to provide Sherine, Joy, and Diego.

After this call, we talked and cried. We were so sad about Selena's difficulties and the loss she felt. We were also determined to protect Matthew. She said some things during the call that, in our opinion, were red flags in her ability to parent. We met with Sherine a few hours later and shared this info with her. She asked us if we were willing to repeat her statements in the court record and we said yes. While we didn't want to see Selena suffer, we realized that we needed to protect Matthew and take care of him.

Over the next few weeks, the biweekly visits stopped. We weren't clear on next steps but received confirmation from Diego that it was not necessary to continue going to the half-way house. He was in the process of meeting with Selena and would let us know when the visits would continue again.

The wheels of justice move slowly. For the next court hearing, DSS would continue forward with their recommendation to provide Selena six more months of reunification services. Lorevic and I were dumbfounded. Why were they not providing recent information about Selena being out of compliance with the court order? Why did they not want to change their recommendation in light of this new situation? Joy informed us that the court tries to give the birth parents the benefit of the doubt and that part of recovery is relapsing. Also, the court had received the paperwork already, and it reflected her progress up until her recent episode.

Lorevic and I were furious. How could they put Matthew at risk of returning him to someone who disappeared for several days? We were protecting and taking care of him every day, but they could consider putting him back in an unsafe situation? Lorevic and I prepared to share the phone call with Selena at the next court hearing. Sherine advised us not to attend the court hearing. We took her advice and stayed away. It was so hard not to be present for this critical juncture in the case. We were anxious to move forward to adoption, yet the court was still considering old information. For the scheduled court appearance, Selena called her lawyer on the court date and requested that the court date be rescheduled due to the death of a relative. We were shocked that the court would postpone the hearing at the last minute. The court hearing was rescheduled for a month later.

In the next month, Diego completed a meticulous evaluation of the case and the circumstances that were unfolding with Selena. He provided us with very little information. Diego told us that he made specific actions and goals for Selena to complete to be considered for parenting. If she failed to meet those requirements, he would change his recommendation. His tone became more upbeat during our visits and other communications. He began to give very subtle hints that he would recommend termination of Selena's reunification services. We were still walking on eggshells and feeling uncertain about our prospects. We had been given this same information a couple of months earlier, and things changed without justification. During this time, Selena had re-emerged and Diego requested visits to comply with the court order. Matthew turned one year old and had spent more than half his life in our care.

His first birthday was an incredible milestone. While Matthew lagged in his growth milestones for height and weight in the first months after he came to live with us, he was doing incredibly well in every other aspect of his life. He had shown tremendous progress in his attachment to his sister and us. His emotions and behaviors were becoming normalized and he was showing less fear and anxiety. He was sleeping better and becoming less upset by things. We celebrated his first birthday with a party of family and friends. After everyone left, and while we were opening gifts, Matthew took his first step. We were elated at his progress and we weren't ready for a mobile toddler. The house needed to be childproofed to keep him safe.

Two weeks after his first birthday, the court hearing for reunification services for Selena would take place. Again, we were told to stay away from the court hearing, which was incredibly difficult. We wanted to tell the court about Matthew's progress and all the reasons he needed to stay in our home. We didn't know what DSS would recommend. We were waiting on pins and needles to hear the outcome.

The day after the court hearing, we received a short email from Diego. He informed us that the court terminated reunification services for Selena, yet we would need to continue to have visits with Selena. We were beyond excited to receive this news and we were sad for the outcome for Selena. While things were starting to look more optimistic about our prospects to adopt him, we still had no legal rights to him. Technically, we were still foster parents. We still had significant hurdles to overcome—determination of permanency plan (also known as a .26 hearing) and termination of parental rights. Each of these steps would happen in several months, and then there would be a waiting period after each court hearing.

The uncertainty and stress took a toll on us, and we were weary, yet our determination grew. While there was a conscious psychological worry about taking care of Matthew's physical and emotional needs, which impacted us, there was an unconscious impact as well. We weren't aware at the time, but on some level, we were holding back from loving him fully. Our unconscious fear of losing him was preventing us from giving every part of our heart and soul to him. A few days after the termination of reunification services, when I was looking at him and changing his diapers, I started to weep. I looked at him for the first time without worrying about losing him. Before, I was grasping at straws to remember every detail and moment with him because I didn't know if it would be the last time. I felt a huge sigh of relief and my heart opened more fully. While we knew he wasn't legally our son yet, we felt hope in a way that we hadn't felt in the past. It was a glorious moment. I also felt tremendous guilt for holding back and not giving him more love during this tumultuous time.

We agreed to do whatever Diego and the court asked of us. We decided to resume visits with Selena because we would do anything for Matthew. This time around, they reduced visits from two times per week to only one visit every two weeks. This change was a considerable relief from a logistics perspective. It's hard enough to take care of a toddler and work, but the additional requirements of twice-weekly visits and work would have been unbearable. It appeared DSS was shifting their position and we were gaining more rights in the situation. They suggested that we could meet on the weekends or evenings after work to not disrupt our lives so much. These visits would happen without supervision from any DSS social workers. While we agreed to visits with Selena, they never resumed due to lack of follow-through on her end.

Diego informed us to start working with the Consortium for Children. They became involved when it became clear that reunification efforts with Selena were not successful and before any court action to terminate parental rights. The Consortium for Children helps negotiate open adoption agreements with the birth parents and adoptive parents. We were elated when we received this email. This news was the first formal step signaling a step forward in our adoption process. We immediately reached out to the organization to schedule a time to begin to mediate an agreement with Selena. We always want our kids to have access to their families of origin. We recognize the incredible importance of understanding their backgrounds and how they came into our lives. We were excited to be taking this step forward. After reaching out, we spoke briefly with the mediator and planned to chat after the holidays.

As the Thanksgiving and Christmas holidays approached, we took a little break from thinking about the next steps in the adoption process. We celebrated our first Thanksgiving and Christmas with Matthew. It was a magical time in our home. There is no greater joy than watching a child wake up on Christmas morning, and we had an incredible holiday season.

After the holidays, we started back to the grind of work, kids, and life. We were balancing a lot of different balls and holding our breath for the next court hearing. We resumed our Sunday routine of going to Most Holy Redeemer Church, fellowship with our church community after mass, and a trip to Collingwood Park for some playtime after mass. Our daughter loves going to church and connecting with other kids in the playroom. Matthew wasn't a big fan of church yet, but he didn't have much of a choice. I loved going to mass to hear the scriptures that helped me make sense of my life and the challenges we were facing. Matthew was about 15 months old and walking like a champ. He moved very quickly and was into everything.

The last Sunday in January, we went to church as usual, except, this Sunday, Lorevic couldn't join us. I took the kids on my own, and we headed to the park after church. Collingwood Park is pretty small and relatively easy to keep track of the kids. As I hovered over Matthew, Kaitlyn became impatient with the lack of attention and wanted to play with me. I engaged with her briefly and turned my attention from Matthew for a moment. When I turned back, he was gone. He climbed the play structure and, in an instant, he stepped off the side of it where there was a pole for kids to slide down. He fell to the ground, and it appeared that he hit his head on the pole. He let out a shriek and started to cry. I freaked out and ran to comfort him. While I was holding him in my hands and trying to calm him down, he became completely silent and almost catatonic. His eyes were open, yet he wasn't showing any expression. Meanwhile, my daughter was playing as though nothing happened.

I panicked. Kaitlyn had an injury as a toddler with lots of blood, but she never behaved in this way. First, my mind raced to think about what to do to make sure he was all right. There was a mother there who came over to help. I quickly gathered all of our belongings, and she helped me get us to the car. We were in the middle of San Francisco, and there were several hospitals within a few miles. I decided to take him to San Francisco General, which is a Level 1 trauma center. In the frenzy of the moment, I texted my husband and he rushed to meet us at the hospital. While driving to the hospital, my mind jumped to the fact that we were still only foster parents and didn't have sole authority over Matthew yet. He continued to be the legal responsibility of the DSS and the Unified Family Court of the Superior Court. I was so worried that social services and the courts would think we were incompetent foster parents and they would consider us negligent for his injury. It was unnerving to be in this position as adoptive parents.

Once we arrived at the Emergency Room at San Francisco General Hospital, we were seen by doctors within 15 minutes. Often ERs have long waits to see providers, but we learned quickly from the staff that they are very concerned about head injuries and kids. Once the doctor started checking Matthew's head injury, I immediately called Joy, Diego, and Sherine. I was terrified that they would consider removing Matthew from our lives because of this accident. I figured that transparency and honesty would be the most important. I immediately started to question if I had done something wrong and if his fall was my fault. Sherine called back right away to check in on us and made a lighthearted comment about kids and injuries as part of the ordinary course of parenting. I felt reassured immediately.

After spending a few hours in the ER and Matthew being observed for a head injury, he was released without any major injuries and we headed home. We were all exhausted by the events over the last few hours and the kids missed their naps, so they were especially cranky. I am pretty sure any injury to a child is exhausting and scary, but the added layer of uncertainty with a foster child makes it that much worse. Foster parenting is stressful and unsettling due to the lack of ownership over the child and situation. As a foster parent, you have all the responsibility and none of the control. When you add on injuries or other challenges, it's overwhelming. In all of these challenging situations, I said prayers to myself and asked God for guidance and support to get me through it.

After Matthew's fall and the scare that followed, I bounced back and started to look ahead to our next court date. In the last few months, we had received positive news about the prospective adoption and we were restless to get everything behind us. We didn't want the stress and uncertainty of others making decisions about his well-being. That's another aspect of foster care that is aggravating. As the foster parents, we knew Matthew better than anyone else and what was best for him. We often had to ask the social workers and attorney for their permission and input in some situations. This feeling undercuts your autonomy and authority over raising the child.

CHAPTER 25

SECOND ADOPTION
FINALIZES

I N MID-FEBRUARY, WE returned to court for the hearing about Matthew's permanency plan. Before this court visit, Selena visited with him for the first time in several months. She was thrilled to see him and all the progress he had made since she had last seen him. He was now walking and was a happy and healthy toddler. It was a bittersweet meeting, as we knew that we were getting closer to adopting him. Since Matthew hadn't seen her in several months, he no longer recognized her. Our bond with Matthew had grown stronger over time and, whenever we were in an unfamiliar space, he stayed close to our sides. He wouldn't go to her and we felt great sadness for her loss and her struggle.

Unlike the last court meeting where we were asked to stay home, for this court hearing, we were required to attend, which signaled a shift in our status. At the end of the court hearing, the permanency plan for Lorevic and me to adopt Matthew was approved. We were elated and couldn't believe the day finally arrived. The court finally recognized us as being the prospective adoptive parents. We still couldn't proceed forward quickly because Selena's lawyer appealed the termination of reunification services and the court had not reviewed the case yet. Sherine told us it was highly unlikely that the court would grant the appeal, but we were forced to wait until that ruling came back. I think I drove Sherine crazy because I kept calling and emailing her every couple of weeks to find out if there was a ruling. I asked her to reach out to the appeals court, but she said that would not be helpful, so we continued to wait. While we were excited that the court recognized us as the adoptive parents, we wanted things wrapped up as quickly as possible.

The next court hearing would take place in May for the termination of parental rights. This event was another major milestone to move us toward adoption finalization. The date couldn't come soon enough for us. During the wait, we celebrated Matthew's first Gotcha Day. We celebrated as a family with a delicious dinner, cake, and candles. We showered him with love and attention. This date would become an essential day in our lives forever, as this was the day that Matthew made our family complete. Kaitlyn was jealous of Gotcha Day because it meant that Matthew celebrated both a birthday and Gotcha Day while she only celebrated her birthday. We explained to her that her birthday was also her Gotcha Day, but she wanted two different days and cakes. We recognized that their different adoption stories would need further explanation as they got older.

For Lorevic and me, the first anniversary of the Gotcha Day took on another meaning. It caused us to reflect on the last 12 months and the turmoil we had endured. The foster-to-adopt process brought us closer together. We had to stay healthy for the kids and be emotionally available for them throughout all this uncertainty. We relied on each other for support, love, tenderness, and understanding. I relied on my belief in God that he was guiding me through this odyssey and loving me through my darkest hours. All of our families, friends, and coworkers were well-intentioned and wanted to help but, despite their compassion, they couldn't understand the burden and stress of the situation. The social workers and lawyers were supportive, but we couldn't be fully ourselves as they were always judging our ability to be good parents. In many ways, the journey was very lonely and isolating. We relied on our friends Elana and Marlene for lots of understanding and support. They heard our cries more than once and were always there to pick us up after a disappointment. The previous 12 months had pushed me to go inside myself and find strength, perseverance, and courage, which weren't always there in the past. The journey built my confidence in myself and made me a better person.

As the May court day approached, we were excited to get the next milestone behind us. A day before the court date, we heard from Diego that the California Court of Appeal denied the appeal for reunification services. DSS could move forward with the termination of parental rights. We were ecstatic about Matthew becoming part of our "forever family," but the court was still the legal guardian. These lurking obligations continued to be a nuisance and put a damper on our excitement. Joy informed us that the case would go to trial in one month. She said we didn't need to go to court the next day because this would be an administrative hearing where they would only be setting a date for the trial. We were elated to be moving one step closer to adoption, but again, we were forced to wait another month to move things forward.

Our next step in the long and weary road to adoption was the termination of parental rights. This period was less worrisome, since it was unlikely for a court to rule in favor of the birth parents. Nonetheless, it was an essential step for our foster son. After termination of parental rights, he was available to be adopted. We attended the court date to demonstrate our complete commitment to taking on full responsibility for their child. We also wanted to chronicle this date in his life to be able to share with him when he was older. The court date was uneventful. We were in the home stretch and beyond excited.

Shortly after this court hearing, the judge assigned a new social worker who specializes in the final phase of our journey, adoption. Thank God for our new adoption social worker, Angie. She had learned of our journey and was 100% motivated to move things along quickly. We met with her in our home soon after the last court date, and we started signing documents. We completed a couple of rounds of paperwork and finally had the disclosure meeting where we learned more about the start of his life and his birth family background. Previously, most information was not shared with us due to confidentiality issues. We were mostly in the dark on so much information.

We started to relish in the fact that we were almost at the end of the road. We began to plan the celebration and send out invitations to family and friends for the adoption finalization ceremony. Once his adoption date was scheduled for September 18, 2017, we scheduled his baptism to coincide with the same weekend. We planned a long weekend for our immediate family to celebrate with us. My mother and sister came from Chicago, and my brother and nephew came from LA. We also planned a big party for all of our friends, social workers, teachers, and caregivers who had been supporting us over the last two years.

At the Adoption Finalization Day with the judge, social workers, lawyers, family, and friends, we cried tears of joy, and our hearts opened up to a world of possibilities. There were lots of tears shed, and we felt a release of worry and fear lifted from our hearts and our lives. In the end, we were elated to have this little boy in our lives. He is the epitome of resilience. He is smart, loving, and affectionate. We cannot believe how far he has come, and we cannot believe how much we have grown and how our hearts have grown wider with love for this child and life.

CHAPTER 26

OUR NEW LIFE

W E STARTED TO plan our future again. We began to think beyond the next court date. We began to live again fully. This change was the beginning of a new life for our family—a life free of social workers, lawyers, paperwork, and worry. The past eight years had been a test of patience and love, a test of stress and ups-and-downs, a test of feeling out of control of our lives and feeling at the whim of others, and a test of faith and resilience. It was finally coming to an end. In many ways, we had put so much of our lives in the hands of others. We felt emancipated from the intrusion of all of these well-intentioned people into our lives. These children were now legally ours while we always knew they belonged with us. We had finally arrived at this point in our lives where our family was complete. We had persevered so much. Through the help of our family, friends, community, and our faith in God, we had overcome tremendous obstacles to create our family. We were free to move onto the task of living, raising our children, and loving them with all our hearts and souls.

Our journey to adopt our children was the most significant lesson of our lives. We learned so much about ourselves and our ability to love in the face of uncertainty and adversity. We learned more than we could have ever learned in any school or work or anywhere else.

Many of the lessons were very hard to grasp at the time, but in hindsight, they were lessons that have prepared us to be incredible parents who can be there for our children for difficult conversations, emotions, and life's challenges. These lessons have given us the confidence and strength to conquer anything that comes into our lives, such as illness, death, or other adversity.

Throughout our journey, resilience and faith gave us the strength to overcome the unknown. Faith in God, faith in love, faith in ourselves, faith in our families, faith in our community, faith in our friends, faith in our social workers and lawyers, faith in our children's caregivers, and faith in the unknown gave us the strength to overcome. Every time we were down, we used this faith to pick ourselves up, keep moving forward, and keep loving. Adoption is not for the faint of heart, but it is a beautiful journey to create a family.

RESOURCES

LGBTQ FAMILY RESOURCES

Our Family Coalition (OFC)'s mission is to advance equity for lesbian, gay, bisexual, transgender, and queer (LGBTQ) families with children through support, education, and advocacy in California. https://ourfamily.org/

Family Equality's mission is to advance legal and lived equality for LGBTQ families, and for those who wish to form them, through building community, changing hearts and minds, and driving policy change. https://www.familyequality.org/

Parents and Friends of Gays and Lesbians (PFLAG)'s mission is to build on a foundation of loving families united with LGBTQ people and allies who support one another, and to educate ourselves and our communities to speak up as advocates until all hearts and minds respect, value and affirm LGBTQ people. https://www/pflag.org

ADOPTION AND SURROGACY RESOURCES

National Council for Adoption's mission is to meet the diverse needs of children, birth parents, adopted individuals, adoptive families, and all those touched by adoption through global advocacy, education, research, legislative action, and collaboration. https://www.adoptioncouncil.org/

AdoptUSKids's mission is to ensure that children and teens in foster care get safe, loving, permanent families. https://www.adoptuskids.org/

Advokid's mission is dedicated to protecting the right of every foster child in California to safety, security, and a permanent home. https://www.advokids.org/

Creating a Family's mission is to strengthen families through unbiased education and support for infertility patients, adoptive parents, foster parents, and allied professionals. https://creatingafamily.org/

Child Welfare Information Gateway's mission is to connect child welfare and related professionals to comprehensive resources to help protect children and strengthen families. https://www.childwelfare.gov/

Fertility SOURCE Companies provides assistance to individuals who are unable to conceive so they can become parents, including matching them with an egg donor, gestational surrogate or both. https://www.fertilitysourcecompanies.com/

Gay Parents To Be® is an informational resource and a starting point for LGBTQ parenting. We strive to provide the best care for LGBTQ couples and individuals as they navigate all of their family building options. https://www.gayparentstobe.com/

ADVOCACY ORGANIZATIONS

Equality California (EQCA)'s mission is to bring the voices of LGBTQ people and allies to institutions of power in California and across the United States, striving to create a world that is healthy, just, and fully equal for all LGBTQ people. https://www.eqca.org/

Human Rights Campaign (HRC) is the largest national lesbian, gay, bisexual, transgender, and queer civil rights organization. HRC envisions a world where LGBTQ people are ensured of their basic equal rights, and can be open, honest, and safe at home, at work, and in the community. https://www.hrc.org/

GLAAD is a national organization that works for fair, accurate, and inclusive representation of the LGBTQ community in the media. https://www.glaad.org/

The National Center for Transgender Equality advocates to change policies and society to increase understanding and acceptance of transgender people. In the nation's capital and throughout the country, NCTE works to replace disrespect, discrimination, and violence with empathy, opportunity, and justice. https://transequality.org

National Gay & Lesbian Chamber of Commerce (**NGLCC**) supports and advocates for diversity and inclusion for lesbian, gay, bisexual, and transgender (LGBT)-owned businesses. https://www.nglcc.org/

LEGAL ORGANIZATIONS

Lambda Legal is committed to achieving full recognition of the civil rights of lesbians, gay men, bisexuals, transgender people, and everyone living with HIV through impact litigation, education, and public policy work. https://www.lambdalegal.org

National Center for Lesbian Rights (**NCLR**) is a national legal organization committed to advancing the civil and human rights of lesbian, gay, bisexual, and transgender people and their families through litigation, legislation, policy, and public education. http://www.nclrights.org/

Transgender Law Center's mission is to connect transgender people and their families to technically sound and culturally competent legal services, increase acceptance and enforcement of laws and policies that support California's transgender communities, and work to change laws and systems that fail to incorporate the needs and experiences of transgender people. https://transgenderlawcenter.org

EDUCATION ORGANIZATIONS

GSA Network is a next-generation LGBTQ racial and gender justice organization that empowers and trains queer, trans, and allied youth leaders to advocate, organize, and mobilize an intersectional movement for safer schools and healthier communities. https://gsanetwork.org/

GLSEN is a US-based education organization working to end discrimination, harassment, and bullying based on sexual orientation, gender identity, and gender expression and to prompt LGBT cultural inclusion and awareness in K–12 schools. https://www.glsen.org/

Our Family Coalition (OFC) works with families, teachers, administrators, and child-serving professionals to create more welcoming schools and agencies to serve LGBTQ families and their allies. https://www.ourfamily.org/schools

HRC's Welcoming Schools Program works to provide training and resources to elementary school educators to embrace family diversity, create LGBTQ and gender inclusive schools, prevent bias-based bullying, and support transgender and non-binary students. http://www.welcomingschools.org/

REFERENCES

Adoption Center, "FAQs." Accessed August 16, 2017. http://www.adopt.org/faqs

Child Welfare Information Gateway. "Adoption Disruption and Dissolution." Accessed October 15, 2019. https://www.childwelfare.gov/topics/systemwide/statistics/adoption/

Considering Adoption. "LGBT International Adoption: Is it Possible?" Accessed October 15, 2019. https://consideringadoption.com/adopting/can-same-sex-couples-adopt/international-gay-adoption

Family Equality Council. "LGBTQ Family Building Survey." Accessed September 5, 2019. https://www.familyequality.org/fbs

Grotevant, Harold D., Ruth G. McRoy, Gretchen M. Wrobel, and Susan Ayers-Lopez, Child Development Perspectives, "Contact Between Adoptive and Birth Families: Perspectives from the Minnesota Texas Adoption Research Project." Accessed October 19, 2019. https://www.ncbi.nlm.nih.gov/pmc/articles/PMC3743089/

Japsen, Bruce. "Branstad speaks with UI fraternity members." *The Daily Iowan*, October 31, 1986.

Savage, Dan. *The Kid: What Happened After My Boyfriend and I Decided to Go Get Pregnant*. New York: Penguin, 2000.

Schmalz, Jeffrey. "March for Gay Rights; Gay Marchers Throng Mall in Appeal for Rights." *New York Times*, April 26, 1993. https://www.nytimes.com/1993/04/26/us/march-for-gay-rights-gay-marchers-throng-mall-in-appeal-for-rights.html

Silber, Kathleen. *Children of Open Adoption and Their Families*, San Antonio, TX: Corona Publishing Company, 1990.

Stone, Geoffrey R. "Remembering the Nazis in Skokie." Accessed May, 15, 2019. https://www.huffpost.com/entry/remembering-the-nazis-in_b_188739

Vacha, Keith. *Quiet Fire: Memoirs of Older Gay Men*. New York: Crossing Press, 1985.

Wrixon, Ann. Independent Adoption Agency Information Session, September 2009.

ACKNOWLEDGMENTS

MANY PEOPLE, RELATIONSHIPS, and life experiences have brought me to this moment when I can share my story about becoming a dad. I am grateful to my family, friends, colleagues, and community who have helped bring my story into reality. It has been through your love and encouragement that I have been able to accomplish this dream.

To my husband, Lorevic, thank you for being my partner on this journey of becoming parents and loving me every step of the way. Creating our family has been a shared quest made possible by your commitment, determination, and patience. For this book, you have shown me unconditional love to dig into our lives and share our story with the public. Throughout, you have been excited about my progress and encouraged me to write from my heart even as I share the most intimate details of our lives. You have given me the time and space to realize my dream of telling our story. Thank you for believing in me. I love you.

To my dear children Kaitlyn and Matthew, thank you for pushing me every day to be better as a father and human being. Every time I get to hold your hands, I feel happiness and love fill my heart and soul. It brings me the greatest joy in the world to be your papa. I love you to the moon and back. Thank you!!!!

To our children's birth parents, thank you for the greatest gifts in the universe, your sacrifice for our benefit, and for trusting in us to be their parents. We thank you for your willingness to be in a relationship with us for the growth and development of our children, and for stepping into the unknown. Thank you for your kindness, trust, and, most importantly, love.

To my parents thank you for helping me to become the man and father that I am today. With your love, support, and teachings, I have been able to come out, live my truth, and create my family. Your early lessons of compassion, giving, and faith, have given me the strength to thrive. To my dad: even though you passed away nine years ago, you are very much present in my life as a role model to lead a purposeful life. I see you every day while parenting my children. To my mom: as I have been writing this book, you have been there every step of the way. Our daily check-ins ground me and provide me inspiration to keep moving forward.

To my siblings Julie, Bob, and Bill, I am grateful for our meaningful relationships and your love and support of my husband and family. I feel blessed to have you all at my side.

To my best friends, Jill Roisen and Jeff McKinney, you have provided me with the foundation for so many things in my life. I am truly blessed to be friends with both of you. You are the loyal and affectionate aunt and uncle to our children and the companions on my lifelong journey. Without your unconditional love and belief in me, this book would not be a reality.

To Jennifer Brown, you emboldened me to share my story. We met at the Professional BusinessWomen of California Conference in 2018, while Jennifer was signing a copy of her first book, *Inclusion: Diversity, The New Workplace & The Will To Change*. She asked me, "Who are you?" and listened closely. At the end of our brief interaction, she said, "Your story needs to be told and shared with the world," which sparked the motivation to begin writing this book. We began a friendship and collaboration. Jennifer, when you asked me to review the manuscript for your second book, I jumped at the opportunity. You found my comments valuable and I gained confidence that I too could be an author. Thank you.

To my longtime friend, Bruce Japsen, who is a trusted advisor and a contributing writer and editor for many publications, including *Forbes*, the *New York Times*, *Chicago Tribune*, and Crain's Business. You have been an integral part of my writing and were instrumental in moving this book into publication. Thank you.

To my Evryman brothers, who embraced me and helped create a space for me to dream and think about the future without holding onto my past. At various points along the journey, I spoke with you about the emotional challenges impeding my ability to share my story. You helped me break through many barriers that allowed me to finish this book. I especially want to thank, Tom Henle, Tim Ridolfi, and Jayme Reynolds, who reviewed an early draft and provided detailed feedback and praise. This helped me keep going to tell a better story. Thank you.

To my business coach, Chris Wilson, I started writing this book before hiring you. While I made good progress on my own, you helped me develop a routine that included rituals and celebrations to acknowledge the progress along the way. These things kept me motivated at those times when I got weary. Our relationship is paramount to writing this book and starting my coaching and consulting business. Thank you, Chris!

To the entire Publish Your Purpose Press team for your encouragement and help. To Jenn Grace, my publisher, for being present and available to talk me through endless aspects of this project. To Karen Ang, who served as my development and copyeditor, while providing critical feedback to make my story/text/book easier and more meaningful for my readers, you were committed to making sure I was telling this story in my own voice. To Niki Garcia, director of operations, for helping me stay on schedule and providing critical support during challenging times. You have all been incredibly patient and supportive throughout the process. Thank you.

To fellow authors, Jennifer Brown, Denise Williams, Marion McGovern, Helio Fred Garcia, and Walt Odets, whose wisdom and practical experiences helped guide me through the publishing process. With each of these warm and welcoming interactions, I gained new insights and felt one step closer to getting my book done. Thank you.

To Ahtossa Fullerton, Adam Tiouririne, David & Janet Van Etten, Carol McDonough, Ruth Abdulmassih, Tiffany Hester, Michele Disselhorst, Claire Chesne, Deb Kopelman, Tom Farnsworth, and Cara Pellegrini. You have been supportive mentors, sponsors, advisors, readers, and friends who have helped me fulfill my dream of becoming an author.

ABOUT STEVE DISSELHORST

STEVE DISSELHORST IS the Founder & Principal of Steve Disselhorst, LLC, which specializes in personal & professional leadership development and consulting for diversity, equity, and inclusion (DEI). Before founding his firm, Steve worked for Genentech, a biotech company, as a Diversity & Inclusion Business Consultant and is a veteran healthcare marketer.

Steve is a co-active trained coach that focuses on an integrated personal and professional leadership development approach. Steve helps clients become emotionally aware and authentic in their lives and work. He works with clients to pursue both short & long term goals and brings awareness to barriers in achieving them and creating accountability. As part of his coaching practice, he works with LGBTQ people interested in creating families.

Steve also provides consulting on DEI in organizations that aspire to create people-first cultures, through trust, honesty, and a deep caring for employees, customers, and the end-user. Whether Steve is creating leadership development programs to advance historically under-represented groups into senior leadership positions, facilitating trainings to improve organizational effectiveness, or designing learning solutions to foster culture change, Steve works with each client to achieve their unique goals.

Steve is available for coaching, consulting, or speaking. Contact Steve if you are ready to transform yourself or your business with a free consultation.

CONNECT ONLINE

www.stevedisselhorst.com

Linkedin: @stevedisselhorst

Facebook: @stevedisselhorst.llc

Twitter: @stevedisselhors

Instagram: @steve.disselhorst

CPSIA information can be obtained
at www.ICGtesting.com
Printed in the USA
LVHW071326201020
669293LV00022B/129/J

9 781951 591113